BERTRAND RUSSELL

BERTRAND RUSSELL was born in England in 1872 and was educated at Trinity College, Cambridge. His long career has established him as one of the outstanding contemporary philosophers and mathematicians. In 1931 he succeeded to the earldom, becoming the third Lord Russell. He was awarded the Nobel Prize for Literature in 1951.

Among his major books are *Principles of Mathematics, Principia Mathematica* (with Alfred North Whitehead), *Introduction to Mathematical Philosophy, The Analysis of Mind, The Analysis of Matter, The Scientific Outlook, Education and the Modern World, Freedom Versus Organization, Power,* and *A History of Western Philosophy.*

THE SCIENTIFIC OUTLOOK

Other Books by Bertrand Russell

Education and the Modern World
Freedom versus Organization
Principles of Mathematics

THE
SCIENTIFIC
OUTLOOK

BY

BERTRAND RUSSELL

The Norton Library
W · W · NORTON & COMPANY · INC ·
NEW YORK

Books That Live

The Norton imprint on a book means that in the publisher's
estimation it is a book not for a single season but for the years.
W. W. Norton & Company, Inc.

PRINTED IN THE UNITED STATES OF AMERICA

Table of Contents

Introduction

To say that we live in an age of science is a commonplace, but like most commonplaces it is only partially true. From the point of view of our predecessors, if they could view our society, we should, no doubt, appear to be very scientific, but from the point of view of our successors it is probable that the exact opposite would seem to be the case.

Science as a factor in human life is exceedingly recent. Art was already well developed before the last glacial epoch, as we know from the admirable pictures in caves; of the antiquity of religion we cannot speak with equal confidence, but it is highly probable that it is coeval with art. At a guess one might suppose that both have existed for some eighty thousand years. Science as an important force begins with Galileo, and has therefore existed for some three hundred years. During the first half of that short period it remained a pursuit of the learned, which did not affect the thoughts or habits of ordinary men. It is only during the last hundred and fifty years that science has become an important factor in determining the everyday life of everyday people. In that short time it has caused greater changes than had occurred since the days of the ancient Egyptians. One hundred and fifty years of science have proved more explosive than five thousand years of pre-scientific culture. It would be absurd to suppose that the explosive power of science is exhausted, or has even reached its maximum. It is far more likely that science will continue for centuries to come to produce more and more rapid changes. One may suppose that a new equilibrium will ultimately be reached, either when so much is known that a lifetime is not sufficient to reach the frontiers of knowledge, and therefore further discovery must await some considerable increase of longevity, or when men become bored with the new toy, become weary of the strenuousness required in the making of scientific advances, and become content to enjoy the fruits of former labours, as the late Romans enjoyed the aqueducts built by their predecessors. Or again it may prove that no scientific society is capable of stability and that a reversion to barbarism is a necessary condition of the continuance of human life.

Such speculations, however, though they may amuse an idle moment, are too nebulous to have any practical importance. What is important at the present time is that the influence of science upon our thoughts, our hopes, and our habits is continually increasing and likely to increase for several centuries at least.

Science, as its name implies, is primarily knowledge; by convention it is knowledge of a certain kind, the kind, namely, which seeks general laws connecting a number of particular facts. Gradually, however, the aspect of science as knowledge is being thrust into the background by the aspect of science as the power of manipulating nature. It is because science gives us the power of manipulating nature that it has more social importance than art. Science as the pursuit of truth is the equal, but not the superior, of art. Science as a technique, though it may have little intrinsic value, has a practical importance to which art cannot aspire.

Science as a technique has a further consequence of which the implications are not yet fully evident, namely, that it makes possible, and even necessary, new forms of human society. It has already profoundly modified the forms of economic organizations and the functions of States, it is beginning to modify family life, and is almost certain to do so to a much greater extent in the not very distant future.

In considering the effect of science upon human life we have therefore three more or less separate matters to examine. The first is the nature and scope of scientific knowledge, the second the increased power of manipulation derived from scientific technique, and the third the changes in social life and in traditional institutions which must result from the new forms of organization that scientific technique demands. Science as knowledge of course underlies the other two, since all the effects which science produces are the outcome of the knowledge which it provides. Man hitherto has been prevented from realizing his hopes by ignorance as to means. As this ignorance disappears he becomes increasingly able to mould his physical environment, his social milieu and himself into the forms which he deems best. In so far as he is wise this new power is beneficent; in so far as he is foolish it is quite the reverse. If, therefore, a scientific civilization is to be a good civilization it is necessary that increase in knowledge should be accompanied by increase in wisdom. I mean by wisdom a right conception of the ends of life. This is something which science in itself does not provide. Increase of science by itself, therefore, is not enough to guarantee any genuine progress, though it provides one of the ingredients which progress requires.

In the following pages we shall be concerned with science rather than with wisdom. It is well to remember, however, that this preoccupation is one-sided and needs to be corrected if a balanced view of human life is to be achieved.

PART ONE

Scientific Knowledge

CHAPTER I

Examples of Scientific Method

I. GALILEO

SCIENTIFIC method, although in its more refined forms it may seem complicated, is in essence remarkably simple. It consists in observing such facts as will enable the observer to discover general laws governing facts of the kind in question. The two stages, first of observation, and second of inference to a law, are both essential, and each is susceptible of almost indefinite refinement; but in essence the first man who said "fire burns" was employing scientific method, at any rate if he had allowed himself to be burnt several times. This man had already passed through the two stages of observation and generalization. He had not, however, what scientific technique demands—a careful choice of significant facts on the one hand, and, on the other hand, various means of arriving at laws otherwise than by mere generalization. The man who says "unsupported bodies in air fall" has merely generalized, and is liable to be refuted by balloons, butterflies, and aeroplanes; whereas the man who understands the theory of falling bodies knows also why certain exceptional bodies do not fall.

Scientific method, simple as it is in essence, has been

acquired only with great difficulty, and is still employed only by a minority, who themselves confine its employment to a minority of the questions upon which they have opinions. If you number among your acquaintances some eminent man of science, accustomed to the minutest quantitative precision in his experiments and the most abstruse skill in his inference from them, you will be able to make him the subject of a little experiment which is likely to be by no means unilluminating. If you tackle him on party politics, theology, income tax, house-agents, the bumptiousness of the working-classes and other topics of a like nature, you are pretty sure, before long, to provoke an explosion, and to hear him expressing wholly untested opinions with a dogmatism which he would never display in regard to the well-founded results of his laboratory experiments.

As this illustration shows, the scientific attitude is in some degree unnatural to man; the majority of our opinions are wish-fulfilments like dreams in the Freudian theory. The mind of the most rational among us may be compared to a stormy ocean of passionate convictions based upon desire, upon which float perilously a few tiny boats carrying a cargo of scientifically tested beliefs. Nor is this to be altogether deplored: life has to be lived, and there is no time to test rationally all the beliefs by which our conduct is regulated. Without a certain wholesome rashness, no one could long survive. Scientific method, therefore, must, in its very nature, be confined to the more solemn and official of our opinions. A medical man who gives advice on diet should give it after full consideration of all that science has to say on the matter, but the man who follows his advice cannot stop to verify it, and is obliged to rely, therefore, not upon science, but upon his belief that his medical adviser is scientific. A community impregnated with science is one in which the recognized experts have arrived at their opinions by scientific methods, but it is impossible for the ordinary citizen to repeat the work of the experts for himself. There is, in the modern world, a great body of well-attested knowledge on all kinds of subjects which the ordinary man accepts on authority without any need for hesitation; but as soon as any strong passion intervenes to warp the expert's judgment he becomes unreliable, whatever scientific equipment he may possess. The views of medical men on pregnancy, child-birth, and lactation were until fairly recently impregnated with sadism. It required, for example, more evidence to persuade them that anæsthetics may be used in child-birth than it would have required to persuade them of the opposite. Anyone who desires an hour's amusement may be advised to look up the tergiversations of eminent craniologists in their attempts to prove from brain measurements that women are stupider than men.[1]

It is not, however, the lapses of scientific men that concern us when we are trying to describe scientific method. A scientific opinion is one which there is some reason to believe true; an unscientific opinion is one which is held for some reason other than its probable truth. Our age is distinguished from all ages before the seventeenth century

[1] See Havelock Ellis, *Man and Woman*, 6th edition, p. 119 ff.

by the fact that some of our opinions are scientific in the above sense. I except bare matters of fact, since generality in a greater or less degree is an essential characteristic of science, and since men (with the exception of a few mystics) have never been able wholly to deny the obvious facts of their everyday existence.

The Greeks, eminent as they were in almost every department of human activity, did surprisingly little for the creation of science. The great intellectual achievement of the Greeks was geometry, which they believed to be an *a priori* study proceeding from self-evident premises, and not requiring experimental verification. The Greek genius was deductive rather than inductive, and was therefore at home in mathematics. In the ages that followed, Greek mathematics was nearly forgotten, while other products of the Greek passion for deduction survived and flourished, notably theology and law. The Greeks observed the world as poets rather than as men of science, partly, I think, because all manual activity was ungentlemanly, so that any study which required experiment seemed a little vulgar. Perhaps it would be fanciful to connect with this prejudice the fact that the department in which the Greeks were most scientific was astronomy, which deals with bodies that only can be seen and not touched.

However that may be, it is certainly remarkable how much the Greeks discovered in astronomy. They early decided that the earth is round, and some of them arrived at the Copernican theory that it is the earth's rotation, and not the revolution of the heavens, that causes the apparent diurnal motion of the sun and stars. Archimedes, writing to King Gelon of Syracuse, says: "Aristarchus of Samos brought out a book consisting of some hypotheses of which the premises lead to the conclusion that the universe is many times greater than that now so called. His hypotheses are that the fixed stars and the sun remain unmoved, that the earth revolves about the sun in the circumference of a circle, the sun lying in the centre of the orbit." Thus the Greeks discovered not only the diurnal rotation of the earth, but also its annual revolution about the sun. It was the discovery that a Greek had held this opinion which gave Copernicus courage to revive it. In the days of the Renaissance, when Copernicus lived, it was held that any opinion which had been entertained by an ancient might be true, but an opinion which no ancient had entertained could not deserve respect. I doubt whether Copernicus would ever have become a Copernican but for Aristarchus, whose opinion had been forgotten until the revival of classical learning.

The Greeks also discovered perfectly valid methods of measuring the circumference of the earth. Eratosthenes the Geographer estimated it at 250,000 stadia (about 24,662 miles), which is by no means far from the truth.

The most scientific of the Greeks was Archimedes (257–212 B.C.). Like Leonardo da Vinci in a later period, he recommended himself to a prince on the ground of his skill in the arts of war, and like Leonardo he was granted permission to add to human knowledge on condition that he subtracted from human life. His activities in this re-

spect were, however, more distinguished than those of
Leonardo, since he invented the most amazing mechanical
contrivances for defending the city of Syracuse against
the Romans, and was finally killed by a Roman soldier
when that city was captured. He is said to have been so
absorbed in a mathematical problem that he did not notice the Romans coming. Plutarch is very apologetic on
the subject of the mechanical inventions of Archimedes,
which he feels to have been hardly worthy of a gentle-
man; but he considers him excusable on the ground that
he was helping his cousin the king at a time of dire peril.

Archimedes showed great genius in mathematics and
extraordinary skill in the invention of mechanical contrivances, but his contributions to science, remarkable as
they are, still display the deductive attitude of the Greeks,
which made the experimental method scarcely possible
for them. His work on Statics is famous, and justly so,
but it proceeds from axioms like Euclid's geometry, and
the axioms are supposed to be self-evident, not the result
of experiment. His book *On Floating Bodies* is the one
which according to tradition resulted from the problem of
King Hiero's crown, which was suspected of being not
made of pure gold. This problem, as everyone knows,
Archimedes is supposed to have solved while in his bath.
At any rate, the method which he proposes in his book for
such cases is a perfectly valid one, and although the book
proceeds from postulates by a method of deduction, one
cannot but suppose that he arrived at the postulates experimentally. This is, perhaps, the most nearly scientific

(in the modern sense) of the works of Archimedes. Soon after his time, however, such feeling as the Greeks had had for the scientific investigation of natural phenomena decayed, and though pure mathematics continued to flourish down to the capture of Alexandria by the Mohammedans, there were hardly any further advances in natural science, and the best that had been done, such as the theory of Aristarchus, was forgotten.

The Arabs were more experimental than the Greeks, especially in chemistry. They hoped to transmute base metals into gold, to discover the philosopher's stone, and to concoct the elixir of life. Partly on this account chemical investigations were viewed with favour. Throughout the Dark Ages it was mainly by the Arabs that the tradition of civilization was carried on, and it was largely from them that Christians such as Roger Bacon acquired whatever scientific knowledge the later Middle Ages possessed. The Arabs, however, had a defect which was the opposite of that of the Greeks: they sought detached facts rather than general principles, and had not the power of inferring general laws from the facts which they discovered.

In Europe, when the scholastic system first began to give way before the Renaissance, there came to be, for a time, a dislike of all generalizations and all systems. Montaigne illustrates this tendency. He likes queer facts, particularly if they disprove something. He has no desire to make his opinions systematic and coherent. Rabelais also, with his motto: "Fais ce que voudras," is as averse from intellectual as from other fetters. The Renaissance re-

joiced in the recovered liberty of speculation, and was
not anxious to lose this liberty even in the interests of
truth. Of the typical figures of the Renaissance far the
most scientific was Leonardo, whose note-books are fas-
cinating and contain many brilliant anticipations of later
discoveries, but he brought almost nothing to fruition,
and remained without effect upon his scientific successors.

Scientific method, as we understand it, comes into the
world full-fledged with Galileo (1564–1642), and, to
a somewhat lesser degree, in his contemporary, Kepler
(1571–1630). Kepler is known to fame through his three
laws: he first discovered that the planets move round the
sun in ellipses, not in circles. To the modern mind there
is nothing astonishing in the fact that the earth's orbit is
an ellipse, but to minds trained on antiquity anything
except a circle, or some complication of circles, seemed
almost incredible for a heavenly body. To the Greeks
the planets were divine, and must therefore move in perfect curves. Circles and epicycles did not offend their
æsthetic susceptibilities, but a crooked, skew orbit such as
the earth's actually is would have shocked them deeply.
Unprejudiced observation without regard to æsthetic prejudices required therefore, at that time, a rare intensity of
scientific ardour. It was Kepler and Galileo who established the fact that the earth and the other planets go
round the sun. This had been asserted by Copernicus,
and, as we have seen, by certain Greeks, but they had
not succeeded in giving proofs. Copernicus, indeed, had
no serious arguments to advance in favour of his view.

It would be doing Kepler more than justice to suggest that in adopting the Copernican hypothesis he was acting on purely scientific motives. It appears that, at any rate in youth, he was addicted to sun-worship, and thought the centre of the universe the only place worthy of so great a deity. None but scientific motives, however, could have led him to the discovery that the planetary orbits are ellipses and not circles.

He, and still more Galileo, possessed the scientific method in its completeness. While much more is known than was known in their day, nothing essential has been added to method. They proceeded from observation of particular facts to the establishment of exact quantitative laws, by means of which future particular facts could be predicted. They shocked their contemporaries profoundly, partly because their conclusions were inherently shocking to the beliefs of that age, but partly also because the belief in authority had enabled learned men to confine their researches to libraries, and the professors were pained at the suggestion that it might be necessary to look at the world in order to know what it is like.

Galileo, it must be confessed, was something of a *gamin*. When still very young he became Professor of Mathematics at Pisa, but as the salary was only fifteen cents a day, he does not seem to have thought that a very dignified bearing could be expected of him. He began by writing a treatise against the wearing of cap and gown in the University, which may perhaps have been popular with undergraduates, but was viewed with grave disfavour by his fellow-professors. He would amuse himself by arranging occasions which would make his colleagues look silly. They asserted, for example, on the basis of Aristotle's Physics, that a body weighing ten pounds would fall through a given distance in one-tenth of the time that would be taken by a body weighing one pound. So he went up to the top of the Leaning Tower of Pisa one morning with a ten-pound shot and a one-pound shot, and just as the professors were proceeding with leisurely dignity to their respective lecture-rooms in the presence of their pupils, he attracted their attention and dropped the two weights from the top of the tower to their feet. The two weights arrived practically simultaneously. The professors, however, maintained that their eyes must have deceived them, since it was impossible that Aristotle could be in error.

On another occasion he was even more rash. Giovanni de' Medici, who was the Governor of Leghorn, invented a dredging machine of which he was very proud. Galileo pointed out that whatever else it might do it would not dredge, which proved to be a fact. This caused Giovanni to become an ardent Aristotelian.

Galileo became unpopular and was hissed at his lectures—a fate which has at times also befallen Einstein in Berlin. Then he made a telescope and invited the professors to look through it at Jupiter's moons. They refused on the ground that Aristotle had not mentioned these satellites, and therefore anybody who thought he saw them must be mistaken.

The experiment from the Leaning Tower of Pisa illustrated Galileo's first important piece of work, namely, the establishment of the Law of Falling Bodies, according to which all bodies fall at the same rate in a vacuum and at the end of a given time have a velocity proportional to the time in which they have been falling, and have traversed a distance proportional to the square of that time. Aristotle had maintained otherwise, but neither he nor any of his successors throughout nearly two thousand years had taken the trouble to find out whether what he said was true. The idea of doing so was a novelty, and Galileo's disrespect for authority was considered abominable. He had, of course, many friends, men to whom the spectacle of intelligence was delightful in itself. Few such men, however, held academic posts, and university opinion was bitterly hostile to his discoveries.

As everyone knows, he came in conflict with the Inquisition at the end of his life for maintaining that the earth goes round the sun. He had had a previous minor encounter from which he had emerged without great damage, but in the year 1632 he published a book of dialogues on the Copernican and Ptolemaic systems, in which he had the temerity to place some remarks that had been made by the Pope into the mouth of a character named Simplicius. The Pope had hitherto been friendly to him, but at this point became furious. Galileo was living at Florence on terms of friendship with the Grand Duke, but the Inquisition sent for him to come to Rome to be tried, and threatened the Grand Duke with pains and penalties if he continued to shelter Galileo. Galileo was at this time seventy years old, very ill, and going blind; he sent a medical certificate to the effect that he was not fit to travel, so the Inquisition sent a doctor of their own with orders that as soon as he was well enough he should be brought in chains. Upon hearing that this order was on its way, he set out voluntarily. By means of threats he was induced to make submission.

The sentence of the Inquisition is an interesting document:

. . . *Whereas you, Galileo, son of the late Vincenzio Galilei, of Florence, aged 70 years, were denounced in 1615, to this Holy Office, for holding as true a false doctrine taught by many, namely, that the sun is immovable in the centre of the world, and that the earth moves, and also with a diurnal motion; also, for having pupils whom you instructed in the same opinions; also, for maintaining a correspondence on the same with some German mathematicians; also for publishing certain letters on the sunspots, in which you developed the same doctrine as true; also for answering the objections which were continually produced from the Holy Scriptures, by glozing the said Scriptures according to your own meaning; and whereas thereupon was produced the copy of a writing, in form of a letter, professedly written by you to a person formerly your pupil, in which, following the hypothesis of Copernicus, you include several propositions contrary to the true sense and authority of the Holy Scriptures;*

therefore (this Holy Tribunal being desirous of provid-
ing against the disorder and mischief which were thence
proceeding and increasing to the detriment of the Holy
Faith) by the desire of his Holiness and of the Most
Eminent Lords, Cardinals of this supreme and universal
Inquisition, the two propositions of the stability of the
sun, and the motion of the earth, were qualified by the
Theological Qualifiers as follows:

1. The proposition that the sun is in the centre of the
world and immovable from its place is absurd, philosophically false, and formally heretical; because it is ex-
pressly contrary to the Holy Scriptures.

2. The proposition that the earth is not the centre of
the world, nor immovable, but that it moves, and also
with a diurnal action, is also absurd, philosophically false,
and, theologically considered, at least erroneous in faith.

But whereas, being pleased at that time to deal mildly
with you, it was decreed in the Holy Congregation, held
before his Holiness on the twenty-fifth day of February,
1616, that his Eminence the Lord Cardinal Bellarmine
should enjoin you to give up altogether the said false
doctrine; and if you should refuse, that you should be
ordered by the Commissary of the Holy Office to relinquish it, not to teach it to others, nor to defend it; and
in default of acquiescence, that you should be imprisoned;
and whereas in execution of this decree, on the following day, at the Palace, in the presence of his Eminence
the said Lord Cardinal Bellarmine, after you had been
mildly admonished by the said Lord Cardinal, you were

commanded by the Commissary of the Holy Office, be-
fore a notary and witnesses, to relinquish altogether the
said false opinion, and, in future, neither to defend nor
teach it in any manner, neither verbally nor in writing,
and upon your promising obedience you were dismissed.

And, in order that so pernicious a doctrine might be
altogether rooted out, not insinuate itself further to the
heavy detriment of the Catholic truth, a decree emanated
from the Holy Congregation of the Index prohibiting
the books which treat of this doctrine, declaring it false,
and altogether contrary to the Holy and Divine Scripture.

And whereas a book has since appeared published at
Florence last year, the title of which showed that you
were the author, which title is The Dialogue of Galileo
Galilei, on the two principal Systems of the World—the
Ptolemaic and Copernican; *and whereas the Holy Con-*
gregation has heard that, in consequence of printing the
said book, the false opinion of the earth's motion and
stability of the sun is daily gaining ground, the said book
has been taken into careful consideration, and in it has
been detected a glaring violation of the said order, which
had been intimated to you; inasmuch as in this book you
have defended the said opinion, already, and in your
presence, condemned; although, in the same book, you
labour with many circumlocutions to induce the belief
that it is left undecided and merely probable; which is
equally a very grave error, since an opinion can in no
way be probable which has been already declared and
finally determined contrary to the Divine Scripture.

Therefore, by Our order, you have been cited to this Holy Office, where, on your examination upon oath, you have acknowledged the said book as written and printed by you. You also confessed that you began to write the said book ten or twelve years ago, after the order aforesaid had been given. Also, that you had demanded licence to publish it, without signifying to those who granted you this permission that you had been commanded not to hold, defend, or teach, the said doctrine in any manner. You also confessed that the reader might think the arguments adduced on the false side to be so worded as more effectually to compel conviction than to be easily refutable, alleging, in excuse, that you had thus run into an error, foreign (as you say) to your intention, from writing in the form of a dialogue, and in consequence of the natural complacency which everyone feels with regard to his own subtleties, and in showing himself more skilful than the generality of mankind in contriving, even in favour of false propositions, ingenious and plausible arguments.

And, upon a convenient time being given you for making your defence, you produced a certificate in the handwriting of his Eminence the Lord Cardinal Bellarmine, procured, as you said, by yourself, that you might defend yourself against the calumnies of your enemies, who reported that you had abjured your opinions, and had been punished by the Holy Office; in which certificate it is declared that you had not abjured nor had been punished, but merely that the declaration made by his Holi-

ness, and promulgated by the Holy Congregation of the Index, had been announced to you, which declares that the opinion of the motion of the earth and stability of the sun is contrary to the Holy Scriptures, and, therefore, cannot be held or defended. Wherefore, since no mention is there made of two articles of the order, to wit, the order "not to teach" and "in any manner," you argued that we ought to believe that, in the lapse of fourteen or sixteen years, they had escaped your memory, and that this was also the reason why you were silent as to the order when you sought permission to publish your book, and that this is said by you, not to excuse your error, but that it may be attributed to vain-glorious ambition rather than to malice. But this very certificate, produced on your behalf, has greatly aggravated your offence, since it is therein declared that the said opinion is contrary to the Holy Scriptures, and yet you have dared to treat of it, and to argue that it is probable. Nor is there any extenuation in the licence artfully and cunningly extorted by you, since you did not intimate the command imposed upon you. But whereas it appeared to Us that you had not disclosed the whole truth with regard to your intention, We thought it necessary to proceed to the rigorous examination of you, in which (without any prejudice to what you had confessed, and which is above detailed against you, with regard to your said intention) you answered like a good Catholic.

Therefore, having seen and maturely considered the merits of your cause, with your said confessions and ex-

cuses, and everything else which ought to be seen and considered, We have come to the underwritten final sentence against you:

Invoking, therefore, the most holy name of our Lord Jesus Christ, and of His Most Glorious Virgin Mother, Mary, We pronounce this Our final sentence, which, sitting in council and judgment with the Reverend Masters of Sacred Theology and Doctors of both Laws, Our Assessors, We put forth in this writing in regard to the matters and controversies between the Magnificent Carlo Sincereo, Doctor of both Laws, Fiscal Proctor of the Holy Office, of the one part, and you, Galileo Galilei, defendant, tried and confessed as above, of the other part, We pronounce, judge, and declare, that you, the said Galileo, by reason of these things which have been detailed in the course of this writing, and which, as above, you have confessed, have rendered yourself vehemently suspected by this Holy Office of heresy, that is of having believed and held the doctrine (which is false and contrary to the Holy and Divine Scriptures), that the sun is the centre of the world, and that it does not move from east to west, and that the earth does move, and is not the centre of the world; also, that an opinion can be held and supported and probable, after it has been declared and finally decreed contrary to the Holy Scripture, and, consequently, that you have incurred all the censures and penalties enjoined and promulgated in the sacred canons and other general and particular constitutions against delinquents of this description. From which it is Our pleasure that you be absolved, provided that with a sincere heart and unfeigned faith, in Our presence, you abjure, curse, and detest, the said errors and heresies, and every other error and heresy, contrary to the Catholic and Apostolic Church of Rome, in the form now shown to you.

But that your grievous and pernicious error and transgression may not go altogether unpunished, and that you may be made more cautious in future, and may be a warning to others to abstain from delinquencies of this sort, We decree that the book Dialogues of Galileo Galilei *be prohibited by a public edict, and We condemn you to the formal prison of this Holy Office for a period determinable at Our pleasure; and by way of salutary penance, We order you during the next three years to recite, once a week, the seven penitential psalms, reserving to Ourselves the power of moderating, commuting, or taking off, the whole or part of the said punishment or penance.*

The formula of abjuration, which, as a consequence of this sentence, Galileo was compelled to pronounce, was as follows:—

I, Galileo Galilei, son of the late Vincenzio Galilei of Florence, aged seventy years, being brought personally to judgment, and kneeling before you, Most Eminent and Most Reverend Lords Cardinals, General Inquisitors of the Universal Christian Republic against heretical depravity, having before my eyes the Holy Gospels which I touch with my own hands, swear that I have always be-

lieved, and, with the help of God, will in future believe, every article which the Holy Catholic and Apostolic Church of Rome holds, teaches, and preaches. But because I have been enjoined, by this Holy Office, altogether to abandon the false opinion which maintains that the sun is the centre and immovable, and forbidden to hold, defend, or teach, the said false doctrine in any manner; and because, after it had been signified to me that the said doctrine is repugnant to the Holy Scripture, I have written and printed a book, in which I treat of the same condemned doctrine, and adduce reasons with great force in support of the same, without giving any solution, and therefore have been judged grievously suspected of heresy; that is to say, that I held and believed that the sun is the centre of the world and immovable, and that the earth is not the centre and movable, I am willing to remove from the minds of your Eminences, and of every Catholic Christian, this vehement suspicion rightly entertained towards me, therefore, with a sincere heart and unfeigned faith, I abjure, curse, and detest the said errors and heresies, and generally every other error and sect contrary to the said Holy Church; and I swear that I will never more in future say, or assert anything, verbally or in writing, which may give rise to a similar suspicion of me; but that if I shall know any heretic, or anyone suspected of heresy, I will denounce him to this Holy Office, or to the Inquisitor and Ordinary of the place in which I may be. I swear, moreover, and promise that I will fulfil and observe fully all the penances which have been or shall be laid on me by this Holy Office. But if it shall happen that I violate any of my said promises, oaths, and protestations (which God avert!), I subject myself to all the pains and punishments which have been decreed and promulgated by the sacred canons and other general and particular constitutions against delinquents of this description. So, may God help me, and His Holy Gospels, which I touch with my own hands, I, the above-named Galileo Galilei, have abjured, sworn, promised, and bound myself as above; and, in witness thereof, with my own hand have subscribed this present writing of my abjuration, which I have recited word for word.

At Rome, in the Convent of Minerva, June 22, 1633, I Galileo Galilei, have abjured as above with my own hand.[1]

It is not true that after reciting this abjuration, he muttered: "*Eppur si muove.*" It was the world that said this —not Galileo.

The Inquisition stated that Galileo's fate should be "a warning to others to abstain from delinquencies of this sort." In this they were successful, so far, at least, as Italy was concerned. Galileo was the last of the great Italians. No Italian since his day has been capable of delinquencies of his sort. It cannot be said that the Church has altered greatly since the time of Galileo. Wherever it has power, as in Ireland and Boston, it still forbids all literature containing new ideas.

---

[1] From *Galileo, His Life and Work*, by J. J. Fahie, 1903, p. 313 ff.

The conflict between Galileo and the Inquisition is not merely the conflict between free thought and bigotry or between science and religion; it is a conflict between the spirit of induction and the spirit of deduction. Those who believe in deduction as the method of arriving at knowledge are compelled to find their premises somewhere, usually in a sacred book. Deduction from inspired books is the method of arriving at truth employed by jurists, Christians, Mohammedans, and Communists. Since deduction as a means of obtaining knowledge collapses when doubt is thrown upon its premises, those who believe in deduction must necessarily be bitter against men who question the authority of the sacred books. Galileo questioned both Aristotle and the Scriptures, and thereby destroyed the whole edifice of mediæval knowledge. His predecessors had known how the world was created, what was man's destiny, the deepest mysteries of metaphysics, and the hidden principles governing the behaviour of bodies. Throughout the moral and material universe nothing was mysterious to them, nothing hidden, nothing incapable of exposition in orderly syllogisms. Compared with all this wealth, what was left to the followers of Galileo?—a law of falling bodies, the theory of the pendulum, and Kepler's ellipses. Can it be wondered at that the learned cried out at such a destruction of their hard-won wealth? As the rising sun scatters the multitude of stars, so Galileo's few proved truths banished the scintillating firmament of mediæval certainties.

Socrates had said that he was wiser than his contemporaries because he alone knew that he knew nothing. This was a rhetorical device. Galileo could have said with truth that he knew something, but knew he knew little, while his Aristotelian contemporaries knew nothing, but thought they knew much. Knowledge, as opposed to fantasies of wish-fulfilment, is difficult to come by. A little contact with real knowledge makes fantasies less acceptable. As a matter of fact, knowledge is even harder to come by than Galileo supposed, and much that he believed was only approximate; but in the process of acquiring knowledge at once secure and general, Galileo took the first great step. He is, therefore, the father of modern times. Whatever we may like or dislike about the age in which we live, its increase of population, its improvement in health, its trains, motor-cars, radio, politics, and advertisements of soap—all emanate from Galileo. If the Inquisition could have caught him young, we might not now be enjoying the blessings of air-warfare and poisoned gas, nor, on the other hand, the diminution of poverty and disease which is characteristic of our age.

It is customary amongst a certain school of sociologists to minimize the importance of intelligence, and to attribute all great events to large impersonal causes. I believe this to be an entire delusion. I believe that if a hundred of the men of the seventeenth century had been killed in infancy, the modern world would not exist. And of these hundred, Galileo is the chief.

II. NEWTON

Sir Isaac Newton was born in the year in which Galileo died (1642). Like Galileo he lived to be a very old man, as he died in the year 1727.

In the short period between these two men's activities, the position of science in the world was completely changed. Galileo, all his life, had to fight against the recognized men of learning, and in his last years had to suffer persecution and condemnation of his work. Newton, on the other hand, from the moment when, at the age of eighteen, he became an undergraduate at Trinity College, Cambridge, received universal applause. Less than two years after he had taken his M.A. degree the Master of his College was describing him as a man of incredible genius. He was acclaimed by the whole learned world; he was honoured by monarchs; and, in the true English spirit, was rewarded for his work by a Government post in which it could not be continued. So important was he, that when George I ascended the throne, the great Leibniz had to be left behind in Hanover because he and Newton had quarrelled.

It is fortunate for succeeding ages that Newton's circumstances were so placid. He was a timorous, nervous man, at once quarrelsome and afraid of controversy. He hated publication because it exposed him to criticism, and had to be bullied into publishing by kind friends. *A propos* of his *Opticks* he wrote to Leibniz: "I was so persecuted with discussions arising from the publication of my theory of light, that I blamed my own imprudence for parting with so substantial a blessing as my quiet to run after a shadow." If he had encountered the sort of opposition with which Galileo had to contend, it is probable that he would never have published a line.

Newton's triumph was the most spectacular in the history of science. Astronomy, since the time of the Greeks, had been at once the most advanced and the most respected of the sciences. Kepler's laws were still fairly recent, and the third of them was by no means universally accepted. Moreover, they appeared strange and unaccountable to those who had been accustomed to circles and epicycles. Galileo's theory of the tides was not right, the motions of the moon were not properly understood, and astronomers could not but feel the loss of that epic unity that the heavens possessed in the Ptolemaic system. Newton, at one stroke, by his law of gravitation brought order and unity into this confusion. Not only the major aspects of the motions of the planets and satellites were accounted for, but also all the niceties at that time known; even the comets, which, not so long ago, had "blazed forth the death of princes," were found to proceed according to the law of gravitation. Halley's comet was one of the most obliging among them, and Halley was Newton's best friend.

Newton's *Principia* proceeds in the grand Greek manner: from the three laws of motion and the law of gravitation, by purely mathematical deduction, the whole solar system is explained. Newton's work is statuesque and

Hellenic, unlike the best work of our own time. The nearest approach to the same classical perfection among moderns is the theory of relativity, but even that does not aim at the same finality, since the rate of progress nowadays is too great. Everyone knows the story of the fall of the apple. Unlike most such stories, it is not certainly known to be false. At any rate, it was in the year 1665 that Newton first thought of the law of gravitation, and in that year, on account of the Great Plague, he spent his time in the country, possibly in an orchard. He did not publish his *Principia* until the year 1687: for twenty-one years he was content to think over his theory and gradually perfect it. No modern would dare to do such a thing, since twenty-one years is enough to change completely the scientific landscape. Even Einstein's work has always contained ragged edges, unresolved doubts, and unfinished speculations. I do not say this as a criticism; I say it only to illustrate the difference between our age and that of Newton. We aim no longer at perfection, because of the army of successors whom we can scarcely outstrip, and who are at every moment ready to obliterate our traces.

The universal respect accorded to Newton, as contrasted with the treatment meted out to Galileo, was due in part to Galileo's own work and to that of the other men of science who filled the intervening years, but it was due also, and quite as much, to the course of politics. In Germany, the Thirty Years' War, which was raging when Galileo died, halved the population without achieving the slightest change in the balance of power between Protestants and Catholics. This caused even the least reflective to think that perhaps wars of religion were a mistake. France, though a Catholic power, had supported the German Protestants, and Henry IV, although he became a Catholic in order to win Paris, was not led by this motive into any great bigotry with regard to his new faith. In England the Civil War, which began in the year of Newton's birth, led to the rule of the saints, which turned everybody except the saints against religious zeal. Newton entered the University in the year after that in which Charles II returned from exile, and Charles II, who founded the Royal Society, did all in his power to encourage science, partly, no doubt, as an antidote to bigotry. Protestant bigotry had kept him an exile, while Catholic bigotry caused his brother to lose the throne. Charles II, who was an intelligent monarch, made it a rule of government to avoid having to set out on his travels again. The period from his accession to the death of Queen Anne was the most brilliant, intellectually, in English history.

In France, meanwhile, Descartes had inaugurated modern philosophy, but his theory of vortices proved an obstacle to the acceptance of Newton's ideas. It was only after Newton's death, and largely as a result of Voltaire's *Lettres Philosophiques*, that Newton gained vogue, but when he did his vogue was terrific; in fact, throughout the following century down to the fall of Napoleon, it was chiefly the French who carried on Newton's work.

The English were misled by patriotism into adhering to his methods where they were inferior to those of Leibniz, with the result that after his death English mathematics was negligible for a hundred years. The harm that in Italy was done by bigotry, was done in England by nationalism. It would be hard to say which of the two proved the more pernicious.

Though Newton's *Principia* retains the deductive form which was inaugurated by the Greeks, its spirit is quite different from that of Greek work, since the law of gravitation, which is one of its premises, is not supposed to be self-evident, but is arrived at inductively from Kepler's laws. The book, therefore, illustrates scientific method in the form which is its ideal. From observation of particular facts, it arrives by induction at a general law, and by deduction from the general law other particular facts are inferred. This is still the ideal of physics, which is the science from which, in theory, all others ought to be deduced; but the realization of the ideal is somewhat more difficult than it seemed in Newton's day, and premature systemization has been found to be a danger.

Newton's law of gravitation has had a peculiar history. While it continued for over two hundred years to explain almost every fact that was known in regard to the motions of the heavenly bodies, it remained itself isolated and mysterious among natural laws. New branches of physics grew to vast proportions; the theories of sound, heat, light and electricity were successfully explored; but no property of matter was discovered which could be in any way connected with gravitation. It was only through Einstein's general theory of relativity (1915) that gravitation was fitted into the general scheme of physics, and then it was found to belong rather to geometry than to physics in the old-fashioned sense. From a practical point of view, Einstein's theory involves only very minute corrections of Newtonian results. These very minute corrections, so far as they are measurable, have been empirically verified; but while the practical change is small, the intellectual change is enormous, since our whole conception of space and time has had to be revolutionized. The work of Einstein has emphasized the difficulty of permanent achievement in science. Newton's law of gravitation had reigned so long, and explained so much, that it seemed scarcely credible that it should stand in need of correction. Nevertheless, such correction has at last proved necessary, and no one doubts that the correction will, in its turn, have to be corrected.

III. DARWIN

The earliest triumphs of scientific method were in astronomy. Its most noteworthy triumphs in quite recent times have been in atomic physics. Both these are matters requiring much mathematics for their treatment. Perhaps in its ultimate perfection all science will be mathematical, but in the meantime there are vast fields to which mathematics is scarcely applicable, and among these are to be found some of the most important achievements of modern science.

We may take Darwin's work as illustrative of the non-mathematical sciences. Darwin, like Newton, dominated the intellectual outlook of an epoch, not only among men of science, but among the general educated public; and, like Galileo, he came into conflict with theology, though with results less disastrous to himself. Darwin's importance in the history of culture is very great, but the value of his work from a strictly scientific point of view is difficult to appraise. He did not invent the hypothesis of evolution, which had occurred to many of his predecessors. He brought a mass of evidence in its favour, and he invented a certain mechanism which he called "natural selection" to account for it. Much of his evidence remains valid, but "natural selection" is less in favour amongst biologists than it used to be.

He was a man who travelled widely, observed intelligently, and reflected patiently. Few men of his eminence have had less of the quality called brilliance; no one thought much of him in his youth. At Cambridge he was content to do no work and take a pass degree. Not being able, at that time, to study biology in the University, he preferred to spend his time walking round the country collecting beetles, which was officially a form of idleness. His real education he owed to the voyage of the *Beagle*, which gave him the opportunity of studying the flora and fauna of many regions, and of observing the habitats of allied, but geographically separated, species. Some of his best work was concerned with what is now called ecology, i. e., the geographical distribution of species and genera.[1] He observed, for example, that the vegetation of the High Alps resembles that of the Polar regions, from which he inferred a common ancestry at the time of the glacial epoch.

Apart from scientific details, Darwin's importance lies in the fact that he caused biologists, and through them, the general public, to abandon the former belief in the immutability of species, and to accept the view that all different kinds of animals have been developed by variation out of a common ancestry. Like every other innovator of modern times, he had to combat the authority of Aristotle. Aristotle, it should be said, has been one of the great misfortunes of the human race. To this day the teaching of logic in most universities is full of nonsense for which he is responsible.

The theory of biologists before Darwin was that there is laid up in Heaven an ideal cat and an ideal dog, and so on; and that actual cats and dogs are more or less imperfect copies of these celestial types. Each species corresponds to a different idea in the Divine Mind, and therefore there could be no transition from one species to another, since each species resulted from a separate act of creation. Geological evidence made this view increasingly difficult to maintain, since the ancestors of existing widely separated types were found to resemble each

[1] Cf. Hogben, *The Nature of Living Matter*, 1930, p. 143.

other much more closely than do the species of the present day. The horse, for example, once had his proper complement of toes; early birds were scarcely distinguishable from reptiles, and so on. While the particular mechanism of "natural selection" is no longer regarded by biologists as adequate, the general fact of evolution is now universally admitted among educated people.

In regard to animals other than man, the theory of evolution might have been admitted by some people without too great a struggle, but in the popular mind Darwinism became identified with the hypothesis that men are descended from monkeys. This was painful to our human conceit, almost as painful as the Copernican doctrine that the earth is not the centre of the universe. Traditional theology, as is natural, has always been flattering to the human species; if it had been invented by monkeys or inhabitants of Venus, it would, no doubt, not have had this quality. As it is, people have always been able to defend their self-esteem, under the impression that they were defending religion. Moreover, we know that men have souls, whereas monkeys have none. If men developed gradually out of monkeys, at what moment did they acquire a soul? This problem is not really any worse than the problem as to the particular stage at which the fœtus acquires a soul, but new difficulties always seem worse than old ones, since the old ones lose their sting by familiarity. If, to escape from the difficulty, we decide that monkeys have souls, we shall be driven, step by step, to the view that protozoa have souls, and if we are going to deny souls to protozoa, we shall, if we are evolutionists, be almost compelled to deny them to men. All these difficulties were at once apparent to the opponents of Darwin, and it is surprising that the opposition to him was not even more fierce than it was.

Darwin's work, even though it may require correction on many points, nevertheless affords an example of what is essential in scientific method, namely, the substitution of general laws based on evidence for fairy-tales embodying a fantasy of wish-fulfilment. Human beings find it difficult in all spheres to base their opinions upon evidence rather than upon their hopes. When their neighbours are accused of lapses from virtue, people find it almost impossible to wait for the accusation to be verified before believing it. When they embark upon a war, both sides believe that they are sure of victory. When a man puts his money on a horse, he feels sure that it will win. When he contemplates himself, he is convinced that he is a fine fellow who has an immortal soul. The objective evidence for each and all of these propositions may be of the slightest, but our wishes produce an almost irresistible tendency to believe. Scientific method sweeps aside our wishes and endeavours to arrive at opinions in which wishes play no part. There are, of course, practical advantages in the scientific method; if this were not so, it would never have been able to make its way against the world of fantasy. The bookmaker is scientific and grows rich, whereas the ordinary better is unscientific and grows poor. And so in regard to human excellence, the belief that men have souls has produced a certain technique for the purpose of improving mankind, which, in spite of prolonged and expensive effort, has hitherto had no visible good result. The scientific study of life and of the human body and mind, on the contrary, is likely, before very long, to give us the power of producing improvements beyond our previous dreams, in the health, intelligence, and virtue of average human beings.

Darwin was mistaken as to the laws of heredity, which have been completely transformed by the Mendelian theory. He had also no theory as to the origin of variations, and he believed them to be much smaller and more gradual than they have been found to be in certain circumstances. On these points modern biologists have advanced far beyond him, but they would not have reached the point at which they are, but for the impetus given by his work; and the massiveness of his researches was necessary in order to impress men with the importance and inevitability of the theory of evolution.

IV. PAVLOV

Each fresh advance of science into a new domain has produced a resistance analagous in kind to that encountered by Galileo, but growing gradually less in vehemence. Traditionalists have always hoped that somewhere a region would be found to which scientific method would prove inapplicable. After Newton, they abandoned the heavenly bodies in despair; after Darwin, most of them admitted the broad fact of evolution, though they continue, to this day, to suggest that the course of evolution has not been guided by mechanistic forces, but has been directed by a forward-looking purpose. The tapeworm, we are to suppose, has become what it is, not because it could not otherwise have survived in human intestines, but because it realizes an idea laid up in Heaven, which is part of the Divine Mind. As the Bishop of Birmingham says: [1] "The loathsome parasite is a result of the integration of mutations; it is both an exquisite example of adaptation to environment and ethically revolting." This controversy is not yet wholly concluded, though there can be little doubt that mechanistic theories of evolution will prevail completely before long.

One effect of the doctrine of evolution has been to compel men to concede to animals some portion, at least, of the merits that they claim for *homo sapiens*. Descartes maintained that animals are mere automata, while human beings have free will. Views of this kind have lost their plausibility, though the doctrine of "emergent evolution," which we shall consider at a later stage, is designed to rehabilitate the view that men differ qualitatively from other animals. Physiology has been the battleground between those who regard all phenomena as subject to scientific method, and those who still hope that, among vital phenomena, there are some, at least, which demand mystical treatment. Is the human body a mere machine,

[1] *Nature*, November 29, 1930.

governed wholly by the principles of physics and chemistry? Wherever it is understood, it is found to be so, but there are still processes which are not completely understood: perhaps in them a vital principle will be found to be lurking? In this way, the champions of vitalism become the friends of ignorance. Let us not, they feel, know too much about the human body, lest we should discover to our dismay that we can understand it. Every fresh discovery makes this view less plausible, and restricts the territory still open to the obscurantists. There are some, however, who are willing to surrender the body to the tender mercies of the scientist, provided they can save the soul. The soul, we know, is immortal, and has cognizance of right and wrong. The soul, if it belongs to the right person, is aware of God. It reaches out after higher things, and is informed by a divine spark. This being the case, it surely cannot be governed by the laws of physics and chemistry, or, indeed, by any laws at all. Psychology, therefore, has been more obstinately defended by the enemies of scientific method than any other department of human knowledge. Nevertheless, even psychology is becoming scientific; many men have contributed to this result, but none more than the Russian physiologist, Pavlov.

Pavlov, who is still alive, was born in the year 1849, and has devoted the bulk of his working life to the investigation of the behaviour of dogs. This, however, is too wide a statement—the bulk of his work has consisted merely of observing when dogs' mouths water, and how

much. This illustrates one of the most important characteristics of scientific method, as opposed to the methods
of metaphysicians and theologians. The man of science
looks for facts that are significant, in the sense of leading
to general laws; and such facts are frequently quite devoid
of intrinsic interest. The first impression of any non-scien-
tific person, when he learns what is being done in some
famous laboratory, is that all the investigators are wasting
their time on trivialities; but the facts that are intellectually illuminating are often such as are, in themselves,
trivial and uninteresting. This applies in particular to
Pavlov's specialty, namely, the flow of saliva in dogs. By
studying this, he arrived at general laws governing a great
deal of animal behaviour, and of the behaviour of human
beings likewise.

The procedure is as follows. Everyone knows that the
sight of a juicy morsel will make a dog's mouth water.
Pavlov puts a tube into the dog's mouth, so that the
amount of saliva to which the juicy morsel gives rise can
be measured. The flow of saliva, when there is food in
the mouth, is what is called a reflex; that is to say, it is
one of those things that the body does spontaneously, and
without the influence of experience. There are many reflexes, some very specific, some less so. Some of these can
be studied in new-born infants, but some only arise at
later stages of growth. The infant sneezes, and yawns, and
stretches, and sucks, and turns its eyes towards a bright
light, and performs various other bodily movements at
the appropriate occasions, without the need of any pre-

vious learning. All such actions are called reflexes, or, in Pavlov's language, unconditioned reflexes. They cover the ground that was formerly covered by the somewhat vague appellation of instinct. Complicated instincts, such as nest-building in birds, appear to consist of a series of reflexes. In the lower animals, reflexes are very little modified by experience: the moth continues to fly into the flame, even after it has singed its wings. But in higher animals, experience has a great effect upon reflexes, and this is most of all the case with man. Pavlov studied the effect of experience upon the salivary reflexes of dogs. The fundamental law in this subject is the law of conditioned reflexes: when the stimulus to an unconditioned reflex has been repeatedly accompanied, or immediately preceded, by some other stimulus, this other stimulus alone will, in time, equally produce the response which was originally called forth by the stimulus to the unconditioned reflex. The flow of saliva is originally called forth only by the actual food in the mouth; later on, it comes to be called forth by the sight and smell of the food, or by any signal which habitually precedes the giving of food. In this case, we have what is called a conditioned reflex; the response is the same as in the unconditioned reflex, but the stimulus is a new one, which has become associated with the original stimulus through experience. This law of the conditioned reflex is the basis of learning, of what the other psychologists called the "association of ideas," of the understanding of language, of habit, and of practically everything in behaviour that is due to experience.

On the basis of the fundamental law, Pavlov has built up, experimentally, all kinds of complications. He uses not only the stimulus of agreeable food, but also of disagreeable acids, so that he can build up in the dog responses of avoidance as well as responses of approach. Having formed a conditioned reflex by one set of experiments, he can proceed to inhibit it by another. If a given signal is followed sometimes by pleasant results, and sometimes by unpleasant ones, the dog is apt to suffer in the end a nervous breakdown; he becomes hysterical or neurasthenic, and, indeed, a typical mental patient. Pavlov does not cure him by making him reflect upon his infancy, or confess to a guilty passion for his mother, but by rest and bromide. He relates a story which should be studied by all educationists. He had a dog to whom he always showed a circular patch of bright light before giving him food, and an elliptical patch before giving him an electric shock. The dog learned to distinguish clearly between circles and ellipses, rejoicing in the former, and avoiding the latter with dismay. Pavlov then gradually diminished the eccentricity of the ellipse, making it more and more nearly resemble a circle. For a long time the dog continued to distinguish clearly:

As the form of the ellipse was brought closer and closer to that of the circle, we obtained more or less quickly an increasingly delicate differentiation. But when we used an ellipse whose two axes were as 9: 8, i. e., an ellipse which was nearly circular, all this was changed. We obtained a

new delicate differentiation, which always remained im-
perfect, lasted two or three weeks, and afterwards not
only disappeared spontaneously, but caused the loss of all
earlier differentiations, including even the less delicate
ones. The dog which formerly stood quietly on his bench,
now was constantly struggling and howling. It was neces-
sary to elaborate anew all the differentiations and the
most unrefined now demanded much more time than at
first. On attempting to obtain the final differentiation the
old story was repeated, i. e., all the differentiations dis-
appeared and the dog fell again into a state of excitation.[1]

I am afraid a similar procedure is habitual in schools, and
accounts for the apparent stupidity of many of the schol-
ars.

Pavlov is of opinion that sleep is essentially the same
thing as inhibition, being, in fact, a general, instead of a
specific, inhibition. On the basis of his study of dogs, he
accepts the view of Hippocrates that there are four tem-
peraments, namely, choleric, melancholic, sanguine, and
phlegmatic. The phlegmatic and sanguine he regards as
the saner types, while the melancholic and choleric are
liable to nervous disorders. He finds his dogs divisible
into these four types, and believes the same to be true of
human beings.

[1] *Lectures on Conditioned Reflexes,* by Ivan Petrovitch Pavlov, M.D.,
p. 342. Translated from the Russian by W. Horsely Gantt, M.D., B.Sc. Published by Martin Lawrence, Limited, London.
   See also *Conditioned Reflexes: an Investigation of the Physiological Activity of the Cerebral Cortex,* by I. P. Pavlov. Translated by G. V. Anrep.
Oxford, 1927.

The organ through which learning takes place is the cortex, and Pavlov considers himself as being engaged upon the study of the cortex. He is a physiologist, not a psychologist, but he is of opinion that, where animals are concerned, there cannot be any psychology such as we derive from introspection when we study human beings. With human beings, it would seem that he does not go so far as Dr. John B. Watson. "Psychology," he says, "in so far as it concerns the subjective state of man, has a natural right to existence; for our subjective world is the first reality with which we are confronted. But though the right of existence of human psychology be granted, there is no reason why we should not question the necessity of an animal psychology." [1] Where animals are concerned, he is a pure Behaviourist, on the ground that one cannot know whether an animal has consciousness, or, if it has, of what nature this consciousness may be. In regard to human beings also, in spite of his theoretical concession to introspective psychology, all that he has to say is based upon his study of conditioned reflexes, and it is clear that, in regard to bodily behaviour, his position is entirely mechanistic.

One can hardly deny that only a study of the physico-chemical processes taking place in nerve tissue will give us a real theory of all nervous phenomena, and that the phases of this process will provide us with a full explana-

[1] Op. cit., p. 329.

*tion of all the external manifestations of nervous activity,
their consecutiveness and their interrelations.*[1]

The following quotation is interesting, not only as illus-
trating his position on this point, but as showing the
idealistic hopes for the human race which he bases upon
the progress of science:

*. . . At the beginning of our work and for a long time
afterwards we felt the compulsion of habit in explaining
our subject by psychological interpretations. Every time
the objective investigation met an obstacle, or when it was
halted by the complexity of the problem, there arose quite
naturally misgivings as to the correctness of our new
method. Gradually with the progress of our research these
doubts appeared more rarely, and now I am deeply and
irrevocably convinced that along this path will be found
the final triumph of the human mind over its uttermost
and supreme problem—the knowledge of the mechanism
and laws of human nature. Only thus may come a full,
true and permanent happiness. Let the mind rise from
victory to victory over surrounding nature, let it conquer
for human life and activity not only the surface of the
earth, but all that lies between the depth of the seas and
the outer limits of the atmosphere, let it command for its
service prodigious energy to flow from one part of the
universe to the other, let it annihilate space for the trans-*

[1] Op. cit., p. 349.

*ference of its thoughts—yet the same human creature, led
by dark powers to wars and revolutions and their horrors,
produces for itself incalculable material losses and inex-
pressible pain, and reverts to bestial conditions. Only
science, exact science about human nature itself, and the
most sincere approach to it by the aid of the omnipotent
scientific method, will deliver man from his present gloom,
and will purge him from his contemporary shame in the
sphere of interhuman relations.*[1]

In metaphysics, he is neither a materialist nor a mentalist.
He holds the view that I firmly believe to be the right
one, that the habit of distinguishing between mind and
matter is a mistake, and that the reality may be considered as both or neither with equal justice. "We are
now coming," he says, "to think of the mind, the soul,
and matter as all one, and with this view there will be
no necessity for a choice between them."

As a human being, Pavlov has the simplicity and regularity of learned men of an earlier time, such as Immanuel
Kant. He has lived a quiet home life, and has invariably
been punctual at his laboratory. Once, during the Revolution, his assistant was ten minutes late, and adduced the
Revolution as an excuse, but Pavlov replied: "What difference does a Revolution make when you have work in
the laboratory to do?" The only allusion to the troubles
of Russia to be found in his writings is in connexion with
the difficulty of feeding his animals during the years of

[1] Op. cit., p. 41.

food-shortage. Although his work has been such as might be held to give support to the official metaphysic of the Communist Party, he thinks very ill of the Soviet Government, and denounces it vehemently both publicly and privately. In spite of this, the Government has treated him with every consideration, and has supplied his laboratory generously with everything that he needed.

It is typical of the modern attitude in science, as compared with that of Newton, or even Darwin, that Pavlov has not attempted a statuesque perfection in the presentation of his theories. "The reason that I have not given a systematic exposition of our results during the last twenty years is the following. The field is an entirely new one, and the work has constantly advanced. How could I halt for any comprehensive conception, to systematize the results, when each day new experiments and observations brought us additional facts!" [1] The rate of progress in science nowadays is much too great for such works as Newton's *Principia*, or Darwin's *Origin of Species*. Before such a book could be completed, it would be out-of-date. In many ways this is regrettable, for the great books of the past possessed a certain beauty and magnificence, which is absent from the fugitive papers of our time, but it is an inevitable consequence of the rapid increase of knowledge, and must therefore be accepted philosophically.

Whether Pavlov's methods can be made to cover the whole of human behaviour is open to question, but at any rate, they cover a very large field, and within this field

---

[1] Op. cit., p. 42.

they have shown how to apply scientific methods with quantitative exactitude. He has conquered a new sphere for exact science, and must therefore be regarded as one of the great men of our time. The problem which Pavlov successfully tackled is that of subjecting to scientific law what has hitherto been called voluntary behaviour. Two animals of the same species, or one animal on two different occasions, may respond differently to the same stimulus. This gave rise to the idea that there is something called a will, which enables us to respond to situations capriciously and without scientific regularity. Pavlov's study of the conditioned reflex has shown how behaviour which is not determined by the congenital constitution of an animal may nevertheless have its own rules, and be as capable of scientific treatment as is the behaviour governed by unconditioned reflexes. As Professor Hogben says:

In our generation, the work of Pavlov's school has successfully tackled, for the first time in history, the problem of what Dr. Haldane calls "conscious behaviour" in non-teleological terms. It has reduced it to the investigation of the conditions under which new reflex systems are brought into being.[1]

The more this achievement is studied, the more important it is seen to be, and it is on this account that Pavlov must be placed among the most eminent men of our time.

[1] Hogben, *The Nature of Living Matter*, 1930, p. 25.

CHAPTER II

Characteristics of Scientific Method

SCIENTIFIC method has been often described, and it is not possible, at this date, to say anything very new about it. Nevertheless, it is necessary to describe it if we are to be in a position later to consider whether any other method of acquiring general knowledge exists.

In arriving at a scientific law there are three main stages: the first consists in observing the significant facts; the second in arriving at a hypothesis, which, if it is true, would account for these facts; the third in deducing from this hypothesis consequences which can be tested by observation. If the consequences are verified, the hypothesis is provisionally accepted as true, although it will usually require modification later on as the result of the discovery of further facts.

In the existing state of science, no facts and no hypotheses are isolated; they exist within the general body of scientific knowledge. The significance of a fact is relative to such knowledge. To say that a fact is significant in science, is to say that it helps to establish or refute some general law; for science, though it starts from observation of the particular, is not concerned essentially with the particular, but with the general. A fact, in science, is not a mere fact, but an instance. In this the scientist differs from the artist, who, if he deigns to notice facts at all, is likely to notice them in all their particularity. Science, in its ultimate ideal, consists of a set of propositions arranged in a hierarchy, the lowest level of the hierarchy being concerned with particular facts, and the highest with some general law, governing everything in the universe. The various levels in the hierarchy have a twofold logical connexion, travelling one up, one down; the upward connexion proceeds by induction, the downward by deduction. That is to say, in a perfected science, we should proceed as follows: the particular facts, A, B, C, D, etc., suggest as probable a certain general law, of which, if it is true, they are all instances. Another set of facts suggests another general law, and so on. All these general laws suggest, by induction, a law of a higher order of generality of which, if it is true, they are instances. There will be many such stages in passing from the particular facts observed to the most general law as yet ascertained. From this general law we proceed in turn deductively, until we arrive at the particular facts from which our previous induction had started. In textbooks the deductive order will be adopted, but in the laboratory the inductive order.

The only science which has, as yet, come anywhere near this perfection is physics. The consideration of physics may help us to give concreteness to the above abstract account of scientific method. Galileo, as we saw, discovered the law of falling bodies in the neighbourhood of the earth's surface. He discovered that, apart from the resistance of the air, they fall with a constant acceleration, which is the same for all. This was a generalization from a comparatively small number of facts, namely, the cases of actual falling bodies which Galileo had timed; but his generalization was confirmed by all subsequent experiments of a like nature. Galileo's result was a law of the lowest order of generality, as little removed from the crude facts as a general law could be. Meanwhile, Kepler had observed the motions of the planets, and formulated his three laws as to their orbits. These, again, were laws of the lowest order of generality. Newton collected together Kepler's laws and Galileo's law of falling bodies, and the laws of the tides, and what was known as to the motions of comets, in one law, namely, the law of gravitation, which embraced them all. This law, moreover, as usually happens with a successful generalization, showed not merely why the previous laws were right, but also why they were not quite right. Bodies near the earth's surface do not fall with an acceleration which is quite constant: as they approach the earth, the acceleration is slightly increased. Planets do not move exactly in ellipses: when they approach near to other planets, they are pulled a little out of their orbits. Thus Newton's law of gravitation superseded the older generalizations, but could scarcely have been arrived at except from them. For over two hundred years no new generalization was found to swallow up Newton's law of gravitation, as it had swallowed up Kepler's laws. When, at last, Einstein arrived at such a generalization it placed the law of gravitation in the most unexpected company. To everybody's surprise, it was found to be a law of geometry rather than of physics in the old sense. The proposition with which it has most affinity is the theorem of Pythagoras, to the effect that the squares on the two shorter sides of a right-angled triangle are together equal to the square on the longest side. Every schoolboy learns the proof of this proposition, but only those who read Einstein learn the disproof. To the Greeks —and to the moderns until a hundred years ago—geometry was an *a priori* study like formal logic, not an empirical science based upon observation. Lobachevsky, in the year 1829, demonstrated the falsehood of this opinion, and showed that the truth of Euclidean geometry could only be established by observation, not by reasoning. Although this view gave rise to important new branches of pure mathematics, it did not bear fruit in physics until the year 1915, when Einstein embodied it in his general theory of relativity. It now appears that the theorem of Pythagoras is not quite true, and that the exact truth which it adumbrates contains within itself the law of gravitation as an ingredient or consequence. Again, it is not quite Newton's law of gravitation, but a law whose observable consequences are slightly different. Where Einstein differs from Newton in an observable manner it is found that Einstein is right as against Newton. Einstein's law of gravitation is more general than Newton's, since it applies not only to matter, but also to light and to every form of energy. Einstein's general theory of gravitation demanded as a preliminary not only Newton's theory, but also the theory of electro-magnetism, the science of spectroscopy, observation of light pressure, and the power of minute astronomical observation, which we owe to large telescopes and the perfecting of the technique of photography. Without all these preliminaries, Einstein's theory could not have been both discovered and demonstrated. But when the theory is set forth in mathematical form we start with the generalized law of gravitation, and arrive at the end of our argument at those verifiable consequences upon which, in the inductive order, the law was based. In the deductive order, the difficulties of discovery are obscured, and it becomes hard to be aware of the immense extent of preliminary knowledge required for the induction which led to our major premise. The same sort of development has happened with a rapidity which is truly astonishing in regard to quantum theory. The first discovery that there were facts necessitating such a theory was made in 1900, yet already the subject can be treated in an utterly abstract way which scarcely reminds the reader that a universe exists.

Throughout the history of physics, from the time of Galileo onward, the importance of the *significant* fact has been very evident. The facts that are significant at any one stage in the development of a theory are quite different from those that are significant at another stage. When Galileo was establishing the law of falling bodies, the fact that in a vacuum a feather and a lump of lead fall equally fast, was more important than the fact that, in air, a feather falls more slowly, since the first step in understanding falling bodies consisted in realizing that, so far as the earth's attraction alone is concerned, all falling bodies have the same acceleration. The effect of the resistance of the air must be treated as something superadded to the earth's attraction. The essential thing is always to look for such facts as illustrate one law in isolation, or at any rate, only in combination with laws whose effects are well known. This is why experiment plays such an important part in scientific discovery. In an experiment the circumstances are artificially simplified, so that some one law in isolation may become observable. In most concrete situations, what actually happens requires for its explanation a number of laws of nature, but in order to discover these one by one it is usually necessary to invent circumstances such that only one of them is relevant. Moreover, the most instructive phenomena may be very difficult to observe. Consider, for example, how much our knowledge of matter has been enhanced by the discovery of X-rays and of radio-activity; yet both of these would have remained unknown but for the most elaborate experimental technique. The discovery of radio-activity was an accident due to the perfecting of photography. Becquerel had some very sensitive photographic plates, which he was meaning to employ; but as the weather was bad, he put them away in a dark cupboard in which there happened to be some uranium. When they were taken out again they were found to have photographed the uranium, in spite of the complete darkness. It was this accident which led to the discovery that uranium is radio-active. This accidental photograph affords another illustration of the significant fact.

Outside physics, the part played by deduction is much less, while the part played by observation, and by laws immediately based upon observation, is much greater. Physics, owing to the simplicity of its subject matter, has reached a higher stage of development than any other science. I do not think it can be doubted that the ideal is the same for all sciences; but it can be doubted whether human capacity will ever be able to make physiology, for example, as perfect a deductive edifice as theoretical physics is now. Even in pure physics the difficulties of calculation swiftly become insuperable. In the Newtonian gravitation theory it was impossible to calculate how three bodies would move under their mutual attractions, except approximately when one of them was much larger than the other two. In the theory of Einstein, which is much more complicated than Newton's, it is impossible to work out with theoretical exactness even how two bodies will move under their mutual attraction, though it is possible to obtain a sufficiently good approximation for all practical purposes. Fortunately for physics there are methods of averaging, by which the behaviour of large bodies can be calculated with a quite sufficient approximation to the truth, although a wholly exact theory is utterly beyond human powers.

Although this may seem a paradox, all exact science is dominated by the idea of approximation. When a man tells you that he knows the exact truth about anything, you are safe in inferring that he is an inexact man. Every careful measurement in science is always given with the probable error, which is a technical term, conveying a precise meaning. It means: that amount of error which is just as likely to be greater than the actual error as to be less. It is characteristic of those matters in which something is known with exceptional accuracy that, in them, every observer admits that he is likely to be wrong, and knows about how much wrong he is likely to be.[1] In matters where the truth is not ascertainable, no one admits that there is the slightest possibility of even the minutest error in his opinions. Who ever heard of a theologian prefacing his creed, or a politician concluding his speeches, with a statement as to the probable error in his opinions? It is an odd fact that subjective certainty is inversely proportional to objective certainty. The less reason a man has to suppose himself in the right, the more vehemently he

[1] The following extract from *Nature* (February 7, 1931) is typical of the cautious attitude of men of science wherever careful measurement is possible:

ROTATION PERIOD OF URANUS.—The two most trustworthy determinations of this period were those made by Profs. Lowell and Slipher at Flagstaff in 1911, and that of Mr. L. Campbell in 1917; the former was spectroscopic, the latter by light-variation. The results were practically identical, 10 h. 50 m. and 10 h. 49 m. respectively. But there was considered to be room for a further investigation, since the indicated probable error of the spectroscopic method was 17 minutes, and the light-variation was not confirmed by several other observers. It may, however, have been produced by a temporary marking. *Pub. Ast. Soc. Pac.* for December contains an account of a new spectroscopic determination made by Messrs. Moore and Menzel. They used a higher dispersion than Lowell and Slipher, also the equator of Uranus is more nearly central on the disc. Their weighted mean is 10 h. 50 m. with a probable error of 10 m.; but in spite of the close accord with the previous results, they do not consider that the period is certainly known within several minutes.

asserts that there is no doubt whatever that he is exactly right. It is a practice of theologians to laugh at science because it changes. "Look at us," they say. "What we asserted at the Council of Nicea we still assert; whereas what the scientists asserted only two or three years ago is already forgotten and antiquated." Men who speak in this way have not grasped the great idea of successive approximations. No man who has the scientific temper asserts that what is now believed in science is *exactly* right; he asserts that it is a stage on the road towards the exact truth. When a change occurs in science, as, for example, from Newton's law of gravitation to Einstein's, what had been done is not overthrown, but is replaced by something slightly more accurate. Suppose you measured yourself with a rough apparatus, and came to the conclusion that you were 6 ft. tall: you would not suppose, if you were wise, that your height was exactly 6 ft., but rather that your height was (say) between 5 ft. 11 in. and 6 ft. 1 in.; and if a very careful measurement showed that your height was (within a tenth of an inch) 5 ft. 11$\frac{9}{10}$ in. you would not consider that that had overthrown the previous result. The previous result was that your height was *about* six ft., and this remains true. The case with the changes in science is precisely analagous.

The part played by measurement and quantity in science is very great, but is, I think, sometimes overestimated. Mathematical technique is powerful, and men of science are naturally anxious to be able to apply it whenever possible; but a law may be quite scientific without being quantitative. Pavlov's laws concerning conditioned reflexes may serve as an illustration. It would probably be impossible to give quantitative precision to these laws; the number of repetitions required to establish conditioned reflexes depends upon many conditions, and varies not only with different animals, but with the same animal at different times. In the pursuit of quantitative precision we should be driven first to the physiology of the cortex and the physical nature of nerve-currents, and we should find ourselves unable to stop short of the physics of electrons and protons. There, it is true, quantitative precision may be possible, but to pass back by calculation from pure physics to the phenomena of animal behaviour is beyond human power, at any rate at present, and probably for many ages to come. We must, therefore, in dealing with such a matter as animal behaviour, be content in the meantime with qualitative laws which are none the less scientific for not being quantitative.

One advantage of quantitative precision, where it is possible, is that it gives much greater strength to inductive arguments. Suppose, for example, that you invent a hypothesis, according to which a certain observable quantity should have a magnitude which you work out to five significant figures; and suppose you then find by observation that the quantity in question has this magnitude. You will feel that such a coincidence between theory and observation can hardly be an accident, and that your theory must contain at least some important element of truth. Experience shows, however, that it is easy to attach too much importance to such coincidences. Bohr's theory of the atom was originally commended by a remarkable power of calculating theoretically certain quantities which had until then been known only by observation. Nevertheless, Bohr's theory, though a necessary stage in progress, has already been virtually abandoned. The truth is, that men cannot frame sufficiently abstract hypotheses; imagination is always intruding upon logic, and causing men to make pictures of occurrences which are essentially incapable of being visualized. In Bohr's theory of the atom, for example, there was a highly abstract constituent, which was in all likelihood true, but this abstract element was embedded in imaginative details which had no inductive justification. The world that we can picture is the world that we see; but the world of physics is an abstract world that cannot be seen. For this reason, even a hypothesis which accounts with a minute exactitude for all known relevant facts must not be regarded as certainly true, since it is probably only some highly abstract aspect of the hypothesis that is logically necessary in the deductions which we make from it to observable phenomena.

All scientific laws rest upon induction, which, considered as a logical process, is open to doubt, and not capable of giving certainty. Speaking crudely, an inductive argument is of the following kind. If a certain hypothesis is true, then such and such facts will be observable; now these facts are observable; therefore the hypothesis is probably true. An argument of this sort will have varying degrees of validity according to circumstances. If we could prove that no other hypothesis was compatible with the observed facts we could arrive at certainty, but this is hardly ever possible. In general, there will be no method of thinking of all the possible hypotheses, or, if there is, it will be found that more than one of them is compatible with the facts. When this is the case, the scientist adopts the simplest as a working hypothesis, and only reverts to more complicated hypotheses if new facts show that the simplest hypothesis is inadequate. If you had never seen a cat without a tail, the simplest hypothesis to account for this fact would be: "all cats have tails"; but the first time that you saw a Manx cat, you would be compelled to adopt a more complicated hypothesis. The man who argues that because all cats he has seen have tails, therefore all cats have tails, is employing what is called "induction by simple enumeration." This is a very dangerous form of argument. In its better forms, induction is based upon the fact that our hypothesis leads to consequences which are found to be true, but which, if they had not been observed, would seem extremely improbable. If you meet a man who has a pair of dice that always throw double sixes, it is possible that he is lucky; but there is another hypothesis which would make the observed facts less astonishing. You will therefore be well advised to adopt this other hypothesis. In all good inductions, the facts accounted for by the hypothesis are such as would be antecedently improbable, and the more improbable they would be, the greater becomes the probability of the hypothesis which accounts for them. This, as we remarked a moment ago, is one of the advantages of measurement. If something which might have any size, is found to have just the size that your hypothesis had led you to expect, you feel that your hypothesis must at least have something in it. As common sense this seems evident, but as logic it has certain difficulties. This, however, we will not consider until the next chapter.

There is one remaining characteristic of scientific method about which something must be said, namely, analysis. It is generally assumed by men of science, at any rate as a working hypothesis, that any concrete occurrence is the resultant of a number of causes, each of which, acting separately, might produce some different result from that which actually occurs; and that the resultant can be calculated when the effects of the separate causes are known. The simplest examples of this occur in mechanics. The moon is attracted both by the earth and by the sun. If the earth acted alone, the moon would describe one orbit; if the sun acted alone, it would describe another; but its actual orbit is calculable when we know the effects which the earth and the sun separately would produce. When we know how bodies fall in a vacuum, and also the law of the resistance of the air, we can calculate how bodies will fall in air. The principle that causal laws can, in this way, be separated, and then recombined, is in some degree essential to the procedure of science, for it is impossible to take account of everything at once, or to arrive at causal laws unless we can isolate them one at a time. It must be said, however, that there is no reason *a priori* to suppose that the effect of two causes, acting simultaneously, will be calculable from the effects which they have severally; and in the most modern physics, this principle is found to have less truth than was formerly supposed.[1] It remains a practical and approximate principle in suitable circumstances, but it cannot be laid down as a general property of the universe. Undoubtedly, where it fails, science becomes very difficult; but, so far as can be seen at present, it retains sufficient truth to be employed as a hypothesis, except in the most advanced and delicate calculations.

[1] See e. g. Dirac, *The Principles of Quantum Mechanics,* p. 130.

CHAPTER III

Limitations of Scientific Method

WHATEVER knowledge we possess is either knowledge of particular facts, or scientific knowledge. The details of history and geography lie outside science in a sense; that is to say, they are presupposed by science, and form the basis upon which it is a superstructure. The sort of things that are demanded on a passport, such as name, date of birth, colour of grandfather's eyes, etc., are brute facts; the past existence of Cæsar and Napoleon, the present existence of the earth and the sun and the other heavenly bodies, may also be regarded as brute facts. That is to say, most of us accept them as such, but strictly speaking, they involve inferences which may, or may not, be correct. If a boy learning history were to refuse to believe in the existence of Napoleon, he would probably be punished, which might, for a pragmatist, constitute sufficient proof that there was such a man; but if the boy were not a pragmatist, he might reflect that if his teacher had had any reason to believe in Napoleon, the reason might have been disclosed. Very few teachers of history, I believe, would be able to produce any good argument to show that Napoleon was not a myth. I am not saying that such arguments do not exist; I am only saying that most people do not know what they are. Clearly, if you are going to believe anything outside your own experience, you should have some reason for believing it. Usually the reason is authority. When it was first proposed to establish laboratories at Cambridge, Todhunter, the mathematician, objected that it was unnecessary for students to see experiments performed, since the results could be vouched for by their teachers, all of them men of the highest character, and many of them clergymen of the Church of England. Todhunter considered that the argument from authority should suffice, but we all know how often authority has been proved mistaken. It is true that most of us must inevitably depend upon it for most of our knowledge. I accept on authority the existence of Cape Horn, and it is clearly impossible that each of us should verify all the facts of geography; but it is important that the opportunity for verification should exist, and that its occasional necessity should be recognized.

To revert to history: as we proceed into the past there is a gradually increasing doubt. Did Pythagoras exist? Probably. Did Romulus exist? Probably not. Did Remus exist? Almost certainly not. But the difference between the evidence for Napoleon and the evidence for Romulus is only one of degree. Strictly speaking, neither the one nor the other can be accepted as mere matter of fact, since neither comes within our direct experience.

Does the sun exist? Most people would say that the sun does come within our direct experience in a sense in which

Napoleon does not, but in thinking this, they would be mistaken. The sun is removed from us in space as Napoleon is removed from us in time. The sun, like Napoleon, is known to us only through its effects. People say they see the sun; but that only means that something has travelled through the intervening ninety-three million miles, and produced an effect upon the retina, the optic nerve, and the brain. This effect, which happens where we are, is certainly not identical with the sun as understood by astronomers. Indeed, the same effect might be produced by other means: in theory, a hot globe of molten metal could be hung up in such a position that, to a given observer, it would seem just like the sun. The effect upon the observer might be made indistinguishable from the effect which the sun produces. The sun, therefore, is an inference from what we see, and is not the actual patch of brightness of which we are immediately aware.

It is characteristic of the advance of science that less and less is found to be datum, and more and more is found to be inference. The inference is, of course, quite unconscious, except in those who have trained themselves to philosophical scepticism; but it must not be supposed that an unconscious inference is necessarily valid. Babies think that there is another baby on the other side of the looking-glass, and although they have not arrived at this conclusion by a logical process, it is nevertheless mistaken. Many of our unconscious inferences, which are, in fact, conditioned reflexes acquired in early infancy, are highly dubious as soon as they are subjected to logical scrutiny.

Physics has been compelled by its own necessities to take account of some of these unwarrantable prejudices. The plain man thinks that matter is solid, but the physicist thinks that it is a wave of probability undulating in nothingness. To put it briefly, the matter in a place is defined as the likelihood of your seeing a ghost there. For the moment, however, I am not yet concerned with these metaphysical speculations, but with the features of scientific method which have given rise to them. The limitations of scientific method have become much more evident in recent years than they ever were before. They have become most evident in physics, which is the most advanced of the sciences, and so far these limitations have had little effect upon the other sciences. Nevertheless, since it is the theoretical goal of every science to be absorbed in physics, we are not likely to go astray if we apply to science in general the doubts and difficulties which have become obvious in the sphere of physics.

The limitations of scientific method may be collected under three heads: (1) the doubt as to the validity of induction; (2) the difficulty of drawing inferences from what is experienced to what is not experienced; and (3) even allowing that there can be inference to what is not experienced, the fact that such inference must be of an extremely abstract character, and gives, therefore, less information than it appears to do when ordinary language is employed.

(1) *Induction.*—All inductive arguments in the last resort reduce themselves to the following form: "If this is true, that is true: now that is true, therefore this is

true." This argument is, of course, formally fallacious. Suppose I were to say: "If bread is a stone and stones are nourishing, then this bread will nourish me; now this bread does nourish me; therefore it is a stone, and stones are nourishing." If I were to advance such an argument, I should certainly be thought foolish, yet it would not be fundamentally different from the arguments upon which all scientific laws are based. In science, we always argue that since the observed facts obey certain laws, therefore others facts in the same region will obey the same laws. We may verify this subsequently over a greater or smaller region, but its practical importance is always in regard to those regions where it has not yet been verified. We have verified the laws of statics, for example, in countless cases, and we employ them in building a bridge; in regard to the bridge, they are not verified until we find that the bridge stays up, but their importance lies in enabling us to predict beforehand that the bridge will stay up. It is easy to see why we *think* it will; this is merely an example of Pavlov's conditioned reflexes, which cause us to expect whatever combinations we have frequently experienced in the past. But if you have to cross a bridge in a train, it is no comfort to you to know why the engineer thought it was a good bridge: the important thing is that it should *be* a good bridge, and this requires that his induction from the laws of statics in observed cases to the same laws in unobserved cases should be a valid one.

Now, unfortunately, no one has hitherto shown any good reason for supposing that this sort of inference is sound. Hume, nearly two hundred years ago, threw doubt upon induction, as, indeed, upon most other things. The philosophers were indignant, and invented refutations of Hume which passed muster on account of their extreme obscurity. Indeed, for a long time philosophers took care to be unintelligible, since otherwise everybody would have perceived that they had been unsuccessful in answering Hume. It is easy to invent a metaphysic which will have as a consequence that induction is valid, and many men have done so; but they have not shown any reason to believe in their metaphysic except that it was pleasant. The metaphysic of Bergson, for example, is undoubtedly pleasant: like cocktails, it enables us to see the world as a unity without sharp distinctions, and all of it vaguely agreeable, but it has no better claim than cocktails have to be included in the technique for the pursuit of knowledge. There may be valid grounds for believing in induction, and, in fact, none of us can help believing in it, but it must be admitted that, in theory, induction remains an unsolved problem of logic. As this doubt, however, affects practically the whole of our knowledge, we may pass it by, and assume pragmatically that inductive procedure, with proper safeguards, is admissible.

(2) *Inferences to what is not Experienced.*—As we observed above, what is actually experienced is much less than one would naturally suppose. You may say, for example, that you see your friend, Mr. Jones, walking along the street; but this is to go far beyond what you have any right to say. You see a succession of coloured patches, tra-

versing a stationary background. These patches, by means
of a Pavlov conditioned reflex, bring into your mind the
word "Jones," and so you say you see Jones; but other
people, looking out of their windows from different an-
gles, will see something different, owing to the laws of
perspective: therefore, if they are all seeing Jones, there
must be as many different Joneses as there are spectators,
and if there is only one true Jones, the sight of him is not
vouchsafed to anybody. If we assume for a moment the
truth of the account which physics gives, we shall explain
what you call "seeing Jones" in some such terms as the
following. Little packets of light, called "light quanta,"
shoot out from the sun, and some of these reach a region
where there are atoms of a certain kind, composing Jones's
face, and hands, and clothes. These atoms do not themselves exist, but are merely a compendious way of allud-
ing to possible occurrences. Some of the light quanta,
when they reach Jones's atoms, upset their internal economy. This causes him to become sunburnt, and to manufacture vitamin D. Others are reflected, and of those that
are reflected, some enter your eye. They there cause a
complicated disturbance of the rods and cones, which, in
turn, sends a current along the optic nerve. When this
current reaches the brain, it produces an event. The event
which it produces is that which you call "seeing Jones."
As is evident from this account, the connexion of "seeing
Jones" with Jones is a remote, roundabout causal connexion. Jones himself, meanwhile, remains wrapped in mystery. He may be thinking about his dinner, or about how

his investments have gone to pieces, or about that um-
brella he lost; these thoughts are Jones, but these are
not what you see. To say that you see Jones is no more
correct than it would be, if a ball bounced off a wall in
your garden and hit you, to say that the wall had hit you.
Indeed, the two cases are closely analogous.

We do not, therefore, ever see what we think we see.
Is there any reason to think that what we think we see
exists, although we do not see it? Science has always
prided itself on being empirical, and believing only what
could be verified. Now you can verify the occurrences in
yourself which you call "seeing Jones," but you cannot
verify Jones himself. You may hear sounds which you
call Jones speaking to you; you may feel sensations of
touch which you call Jones bumping into you. If he has
not lately had a bath, you may also have olfactory sensations of which you suppose him to be the source. If you
have been impressed by this argument, you may address
him as if he were at the other end of the telephone, and
say, "Are you there?" And you may subsequently hear
the words: "Yes, you idiot, can't you see me?" But if you
regard these as affording evidence that he is there, you
have missed the point of the argument. The point is that
Jones is a convenient hypothesis by means of which certain of your own sensations can be collected into a bundle;
but what really makes them belong together is not their
common hypothetical origin, but certain resemblances
and causal affinities which they have to each other. These
remain, even if their common origin is mythical. When

you see a man in the cinema, you know that he does not exist when he is off the stage, though you suppose that there was an original who did exist continuously. But why should you make this supposition? Why should not Jones be like the man you see at the cinema? He may get annoyed with you if you suggest such an idea, but he will be powerless to disprove it, since he cannot give you any experience of what he is doing when you do not experience him.

Is there any way of proving that there are occurrences other than those that you yourself experience? This is a question of some emotional interest, but the theoretical physicist of the present day would consider it unimportant. "My formulae," he would say, "are concerned to provide causal laws connecting my sensations. In the statement of these causal laws I may employ hypothetical entities; but the question whether these entities are more than hypothetical is otiose, since it lies outside the sphere of possible verification." At a pinch, he may admit that other physicists exist, since he wishes to use their results; and, having admitted physicists, he may be led by politeness to admit students of other sciences. He may, in fact, form an argument by analogy to prove that, just as his body is connected with his thoughts, so bodies closely resembling his own are probably also connected with thoughts. It may be questioned how much strength there is in this argument; but, even if it be admitted, it does not allow us to conclude that the sun and stars exist, or, indeed, any lifeless matter. We are, in fact, led to the position of Berkeley, according to which only thoughts exist. Berkeley saved the universe and the permanence of bodies by regarding them as God's thoughts, but this was only a wish-fulfilment, not logical thinking. However, as he was at once a bishop and an Irishman, we ought not to be too hard on him. The fact is that science started with a large amount of what Santayana calls "animal faith," which is, in fact, thought dominated by the principle of the conditioned reflex. It was this animal faith that enabled physicists to believe in a world of matter. Gradually they have turned traitor, like men who, from studying the history of kings, have become republicans. The physicists of our day no longer believe in matter. That in itself, however, would be no great loss, provided we could still have a large and varied external world, but unfortunately they have not supplied us with any reason for believing in a non-material external world.

The problem is not essentially one for the physicist, but for the logician. It is, in essence, a simple one, namely: are circumstances ever such as to enable us, from a set of known events, to infer that some other event has occurred, is occurring, or will occur? Or, if we cannot make such an inference with certainty, can we ever make it with any high degree of probability, or at any rate with a probability greater than a half? If the answer to this question is in the affirmative, we may be justified in believing, as we all do in fact believe, in the occurrence of events which we have not personally experienced. If the answer is in the negative, we can never be justified in our belief. Logicians have hardly ever considered this question in its naked simplicity, and I do not know of any clear answer to it. Until an answer is forthcoming, one way or another, the question must remain an open one, and our faith in the external world must be merely animal faith.

(3) *The Abstractness of Physics.*—Even allowing that the sun, the stars, and the material world generally, are not a figment of our imagination, or a set of convenient coefficients in our equations, what can be said about them is extraordinarily abstract, much more so than appears from the language employed by physicists when they attempt to be intelligible. The space and time that they deal with are not the space and time of our experience. The orbits of the planets do not resemble the pictorial ellipses which we see drawn in charts of the solar system, except in certain quite abstract properties. It is possible that the relation of contiguity which occurs in our experience may be extended to the bodies of the physical world, but other relations known in experience are not themselves known to exist in the physical world. The most that can be known, and that only on the most hopeful view, is that there are certain relations in the physical world which share certain abstract logical characteristics with the relations that we know. The characteristics which they share are those that can be expressed mathematically, not those that distinguish them imaginatively from other relations. Take, for example, what there is in common between a gramophone record and the music that it plays; the two share certain structural properties which can be expressed in abstract

terms, but they do not share any properties that are obvious to the senses. In virtue of their structural similarity, the one can cause the other. Similarly, a physical world sharing the structure of our sensible world can cause it, even though it may resemble it in nothing except structure. At best, therefore, we can only know concerning the physical world such properties as the gramophone record and the music have in common, not such as distinguish them one from the other. Ordinary language is totally unsuited for expressing what physics really asserts, since the words of everyday life are not sufficiently abstract. Only mathematics and mathematical logic can say as little as the physicist means to say. As soon as he translates his symbols into words, he inevitably says something much too concrete, and gives his readers a cheerful impression of something imaginable and intelligible, which is much more pleasant and everyday than what he is trying to convey.

Many people have a passionate hatred of abstraction, chiefly, I think, because of its intellectual difficulty; but as they do not wish to give this reason, they invent all sorts of others that sound grand. They say that all reality is concrete, and that in making abstractions we are leaving out the essential. They say that all abstraction is falsification, and that as soon as you have left out any aspect of something actual you have exposed yourself to the risk of fallacy in arguing from its remaining aspects alone. Those who argue in this way are, in fact, concerned with matters quite other than those that concern science. From the æsthetic point of view, for example, abstraction is likely to be wholly misleading. The music may be beautiful, while the gramophone record is æsthetically null; from the point of view of imaginative vision, such as an epic poet may desire in writing of the creation, the abstract knowledge offered by physics is not satisfying. He wants to know what God saw when He looked upon the world and saw that it was good; he cannot be satisfied with formulae giving the abstract logical properties of the relations among the different parts of what God saw. But scientific thought is different from this. It is essentially power-thought—the sort of thought, that is to say, whose purpose, conscious or unconscious, is to give power to its possessor. Now power is a causal concept, and to obtain power over any given material, one need only understand the causal laws to which it is subject. This is an essentially abstract matter, and the more irrelevant details we can omit from our purview, the more powerful our thoughts will become. The same sort of thing can be illustrated in the economic sphere. The cultivator, who knows every corner of his farm, has a concrete knowledge of wheat, and makes very little money; the railway which carries his wheat views it in a slightly more abstract way, and makes rather more money; the Stock Exchange manipulator, who knows it only in its purely abstract aspect of something which may go up or down, is, in his way, as remote from concrete reality as the physicist, and he, of all those concerned in the economic sphere, makes the most money and has the most power. So it is with science, though the power which the man of science seeks is more remote and impersonal than that which is sought on the Stock Exchange.

The extreme abstractness of modern physics makes it difficult to understand, but gives to those who can understand it a grasp of the world as a whole, a sense of its structure and mechanism, which no less abstract apparatus could possibly supply. The power of using abstractions is the essence of intellect, and with every increase in abstraction the intellectual triumphs of science are enhanced.

CHAPTER IV

Scientific Metaphysics [1]

I T is a curious fact that, just when the man in street has begun to believe thoroughly in science, the man in the laboratory has begun to lose his faith. When I was young, most physicists entertained not the slightest doubt that the laws of physics give us real information about the motions of bodies, and that the physical world does really consist of the sort of entities that appear in the physicists' equations. The philosophers, it is true, threw doubt upon this view and have done so ever since the time of Berkeley, but since their criticism never attached itself to any point in the detailed procedure of science, it could be ignored by scientists, and was in fact ignored. Nowadays, matters are quite different; the revolutionary ideas of the philosophy of physics have come from the physicists themselves, and are the outcome of careful experiments. The new philosophy of physics is humble and stammering, where the old philosophy was proud and dictatorial. It is, I suppose, natural that every man should fill the vacuum left by the disappearance of belief in physical laws as best he may, and that he should use for this pur-

[1] Part of this chapter is based upon an article called "What I Believe," which appeared in *The Nation* for April 29, 1931.

pose any odds and ends of unfounded belief which had previously no room to expand. When the robustness of the Catholic faith decayed at the time of the Renaissance, it tended to be replaced by astrology and necromancy, and in like manner we must expect the decay of the scientific faith to lead to a recrudescence of pre-scientific superstitions.

So long as we do not inquire too closely what the scientist really means, he seems to be presenting us with a more and more imposing edifice of knowledge. This is especially the case in astronomy. The Milky Way, as everyone knows, consists of all the stars in our neighbourhood. Light travels 186,000 miles in a second; the distance that it travels in a year is known as a light year; the distance of the nearest star is about four light years; the distance of the furthest stars in the Milky Way is about 220,000 light years. Telescopes reveal about two million systems of stars each analogous to the Milky Way, some at distances of over a hundred million light years. The universe is thus of a considerable size, but it is not supposed to be infinite. It is supposed that if you travelled long enough in a straight line you would ultimately return to your starting-point, like a ship going round the world. There is, however, some reason to think that the universe is continually growing bigger, like a soap-bubble while it is being blown. An eminent astronomer, Arthur Haas, suggests that the universe at some not infinitely remote epoch had a radius of 1,200 million light years, but that its radius is doubled every 1,400 million

years, that is within a time shorter even than the age of
many minerals, not to speak of astronomical estimates of
the age of the sun (*Nature*, February 7, 1931). This
sounds quite impressive, but the scientists themselves are
by no means persuaded that there is any objective reality
about the large numbers in which they deal. I do not
mean by this that they think the laws they are enunciating
untrue; I mean rather that these laws are capable of an
interpretation which turns the abysses of astronomical
space into mere auxiliary concepts, which are useful in the
calculations by means of which we connect one real occurrence with another. Sometimes it would seem as if
astronomers considered that the only real occurrences
with which they are concerned are the observations of
astronomers.

Whoever wishes to know how and why scientific faith
is decaying cannot do better than read Eddington's
Gifford lectures entitled *The Nature of the Physical
World*. He will learn there that physics is divided into
three departments. The first contains all the laws of classical physics, such as the conservation of energy and momentum and the law of gravitation. All these, according
to Professor Eddington, boil down to nothing but conventions as to measurement; true, the laws they state are
universal, but so is the law that there are three feet in a
yard, which, according to him, is just as informative concerning the course of nature. The second department of
physics is concerned with large aggregates and the laws
of chance. Here we do not attempt to prove that such and

such an·event is impossible, but only that it is wildly improbable. The third department of physics, which is the most modern, is the quantum theory, and this is the most disturbing of all, since it seems to show that perhaps the law of causality, in which science has hitherto implicitly believed, cannot be applied to the doings of individual electrons. I shall say a few words about each of these three matters in turn.

To begin with classical physics. Newton's law of gravitation, as everyone knows, was somewhat modified by Einstein, and the modification was experimentally confirmed. But if Eddington's view is right, this experimental confirmation does not have the significance that one would naturally attribute to it. After considering three possible views as to what the law of gravitation asserts about the motion of the earth round the sun, Eddington plumps for a fourth, to the effect that "the earth goes anyhow it likes"; that is to say, the law of gravitation tells us absolutely nothing about the way the earth moves. He admits that this view is paradoxical, but he says:

"The key to the paradox is that we ourselves, our conventions, the kind of thing that attracts our interest, are much more concerned than we realize in any account we give of how the objects of the physical world are behaving. And so an object which, viewed through our frame of conventions, may seem to be behaving in a very special and remarkable way, viewed according to another set of conventions, may be doing nothing to excite particular comment."

I must confess that I find this view a very difficult one; respect for Eddington prevents me from saying that it is untrue, but there are various points in his argument which I have difficulty in following. Of course, all the practical consequences which we deduce from the abstract theory, as, for example, that we shall perceive daylight at certain times and not at certain other times, lie outside the scheme of official physics, which never reaches our sensations at all. I cannot but suspect, however, that official physics is just a little bit too official in Eddington's hands, and that it will not be impossible to allow it a little more significance than it has in his interpretation. However that may be, it is an important sign of the times that one of the leading exponents of scientific theory should advance so modest an opinion.

I come now to the statistical part of physics, which is concerned with the study of large aggregates. Large aggregates behave almost exactly as they were supposed to do before the quantum theory was invented, so that in regard to them the older physics is very nearly right. There is, however, one supremely important law which is only statistical; this is the second law of thermodynamics. It states, roughly speaking, that the world is growing continuously more disorderly. Eddington illustrates it by what happens when you shuffle a pack of cards. The pack of cards comes from the makers with the cards arranged in their proper order; after you have shuffled them, this order is lost, and it is in the highest degree improbable that it will ever be restored by subsequent shuffling. It is this sort of thing that makes the difference between past and future. In the rest of theoretical physics we are dealing with processes that are reversible; that is to say, where the laws of physics show that it is possible for a material system to pass from state A at one time to state B at another, the opposite transition will be equally possible according to these same laws. But where the second law of thermodynamics comes in, this is not the case. Eddington enunciates the law as follows: "Whenever anything happens that cannot be undone, it is always reducible to the introduction of a random element analogous to that introduced by shuffling." This law, unlike most of the laws of physics, is concerned only with probabilities. To take our previous illustration: it is of course possible that if you shuffle a pack of cards long enough, the cards may happen to get into the right order by chance. This is very unlikely, but it is far less unlikely than the orderly arrangement of many millions of molecules by chance. Eddington gives the following illustration: suppose a vessel divided into two equal parts by a partition, and suppose that in one part there is air, while in the other there is a vacuum; then a door in the partition is opened and the air spreads itself evenly through the whole vessel. It might happen by chance that at some future time the molecules of the air in the course of their random movements would all find themselves again in the partition in which they originally were. This is not impossible; it is only improbable, but it is *very* improbable. "If I let my fingers wander idly over the keys of a typewriter it *might* happen that my screed made an intelligible sentence. If an army of monkeys were strumming on typewriters they *might* write all the books in the British Museum. The chance of their doing so is decidedly more favourable than the chance of the molecules returning to one half of the vessel."

There are an immense number of illustrations of the same kind of thing. For example, if you drop one drop of ink into a glass of clear water it will gradually diffuse itself throughout the glass. It might happen by chance that it would afterwards collect itself again into a drop, but we should certainly regard it as a miracle if this happened. When a hot body and a cold body are put in contact, we all know that the hot body cools and the cold body gets warm until the two reach the same temperature, but this also is only a law of probability. It might happen that a kettle filled with water put on the fire would freeze instead of boiling; this also is not shown to be impossible by any of the laws of physics, it is only shown to be highly improbable by the second law of thermodynamics. This law states, speaking generally, that the universe tends towards democracy, and that when it has achieved that state, it will be incapable of doing anything more. It seems that the world was created at some not infinitely remote date, and was then far more full of inequalities than it is now, but from the moment of creation it has been continually running down, and will ultimately stop for all practical purposes unless it is again wound up. Eddington for some reason does not like the idea that it can be wound up again, but prefers to think that the world drama is only to be performed once, in spite of the fact that it must end in æons of boredom, in the course of which the whole audience will gradually go to sleep.

Quantum theory, which is concerned with individual atoms and electrons, is still in a state of rapid development, and is probably far from its final form. In the hands of Heisenberg, Schrödinger and Co., it has become more disturbing and more revolutionary than the theory of relativity ever was. Eddington expounds its recent development in a manner which conveys more of it to the non-mathematical reader than I should have supposed possible. It is profoundly disturbing to the prejudices which have governed physics since the time of Newton. The most painful thing about it from this point of view is that, as mentioned above, it throws doubt upon the universality of causality; the view at present is that perhaps atoms have a certain amount of free will, so that their behaviour, even in theory, is not wholly subject to law. Moreover, some things which we thought definite, at least in theory, have quite ceased to be so. There is what is called the "principle of indeterminacy": this states that "a particle may have position or it may have velocity, but it cannot in any exact sense have both"; that is to say, if you know where you are, you cannot tell how fast you are moving, and if you know how fast you are moving, you cannot tell where you are. This cuts at the root of traditional physics, in which position and velocity were fundamental. You can only see an electron when it emits light, and it only emits light when it jumps, so that to see where it was you have to make it go elsewhere. This is interpreted by some writers as a breakdown of physical determinism, and is utilized by Eddington in his concluding chapters to rehabilitate free will.

Eddington proceeds to base optimistic and pleasant conclusions upon the scientific nescience which he has expounded in previous pages. This optimism is based upon the time-honoured principle that anything which cannot be proved untrue may be assumed to be true, a principle whose falsehood is proved by the fortunes of bookmakers. If we discard this principle, it is difficult to see what ground for cheerfulness modern physics provides. It tells us that the universe is running down, and if Eddington is right, it tells us practically nothing else, since all the rest is merely rules of the game.

As Eddington himself has pointed out, in spite of evolution, which is introducing increasing organization into one little corner of the universe, there is, on the whole, a general loss of organization which will finally swallow up the organization due to evolution. In the end, he says, the whole universe will reach a state of complete disorganization which will be the end of the world. At this stage the universe will consist of a uniform mass at a uniform temperature. Nothing further will happen except that the universe will gradually swell. It speaks well for his temperamental cheerfulness that he should find in this view a basis for optimism.

From a pragmatic or political point of view probably

the most important thing about such a theory of physics is that it will destroy, if it becomes widespread, that faith in science which has been the only constructive creed of modern times, and the source of practically all change both for good and for evil. The eighteenth and nineteenth centuries had a philosophy of natural law based upon Newton. The law was supposed to imply a Lawgiver, though as time went on this inference was less emphasized, but in any case the universe was orderly and predictable. By learning nature's laws we could hope to manipulate nature, and thus science became the source of power. This is still the outlook of most energetic practical men, but it is no longer the outlook of some among the men of science. The world, according to them, is a more higgledy-piggledy and haphazard affair than it was thought to be. And they know much less about it than was thought to be known by their predecessors in the eighteenth and nineteenth centuries. Perhaps the scientific scepticism of which Eddington is an exponent may lead in the end to the collapse of the scientific era, just as the theological scepticism of the Renaissance has led gradually to the collapse of the theological era. I suppose that machines will survive the collapse of science, just as parsons have survived the collapse of theology, but in the one case as in the other they will cease to be viewed with reverence and awe.

What, in these circumstances, has science to contribute to metaphysics? Academic philosophers, ever since the time of Parmenides, have believed that the world is a unity. This view has been taken over from them by clergymen and journalists, and its acceptance has been considered the touchstone of wisdom. The most fundamental of my intellectual beliefs is that this is rubbish. I think the universe is all spots and jumps, without unity, without continuity, without coherence or orderliness or any of the other properties that governesses love. Indeed, there is little but prejudice and habit to be said for the view that there is a world at all. Physicists have recently advanced opinions which should have led them to agree with the foregoing remarks; but they have been so pained by the conclusions to which logic would have led them that they have been abandoning logic for theology in shoals. Every day some new physicist publishes a new pious volume to conceal from himself and others the fact that in his scientific capacity he has plunged the world into unreason and unreality. To take an illustration: What are we to think of the sun? He used to be the glorious lamp of Heaven, a golden-haired god, a being to be worshipped by Zoroastrians and Aztecs and Incas. There is some reason to think that the doctrines of Zoroaster inspired Kepler's heliocentric cosmogony. But now the sun is nothing but waves of probability. If you ask what it is that is probable, or in what ocean the waves travel, the physicist, like the Mad Hatter, replies: "I have had enough of this; supppose we change the subject." If, however, you press him, he will say that the waves are in his formulae, and his formulae are in his head, from which, however, you must not infer that the waves are in his head. To speak seriously: such orderliness as we appear to find in the external world is held by many to be due to our own passion for pigeon-holes, and they maintain that it is quite doubtful whether there are such things as laws of nature. It is a curious sign of the times that religious apologists welcome this view. In the eighteenth century they welcomed the reign of law, since they thought that laws implied a Lawgiver, but religious apologists in the present day seem to be of opinion that a world created by a Deity must be irrational, on the ground, apparently, that they themselves have been made in God's image.[1] The reconciliation of religion and science which professors proclaim and Bishops acclaim rests, in fact, though subconsciously, on grounds of quite another sort, and might be set forth in the following practical syllogism: science depends upon endowments, and endowments are threatened by Bolshevism; therefore science is threatened by Bolshevism; but religion is also threatened by Bolshevism; therefore religion and science are allies. It follows, of course, that science, if pursued with sufficient profundity, reveals the existence of a God. Nothing so logical as this penetrates, however, to the consciousness of the pious professors.

The odd thing is that, at the very moment when

[1] This modern point of view is by no means universal, even among physicists. Millikan, for example, speaking of Galileo's work, says: "Through it mankind began to know a God not of caprice and whim, such as were all the gods of the ancient world, but a God who works through law." (*Science and Religion*, 1929, p. 39.) Most modern physicists, however, show a preference for caprice and whim.

physics, which is the fundamental science, is undermining the whole structure of applied reason and presenting us with a world of unreal and fantastic dreams in place of the Newtonian order and solidity, applied science is becoming peculiarly useful and more able than ever to give results of value to human life. There is here a paradox, of which possibly the intellectual solution may be found hereafter, or, equally possibly, no solution may exist. The fact is that science plays two quite distinct rôles: on the one hand as a metaphysic, and on the other hand as educated common sense. As a metaphysic it has been undermined by its own success. Mathematical technique is now so powerful that it can find a formula for even the most erratic world. Plato and Sir James Jeans think that because geometry applies to the world, God must have made the world on a geometrical pattern, but the mathematical logician suspects that God could not have made a world containing many things without exposing it to the skill of the geometer. In fact, the applicability of geometry to the physical world has ceased to be a fact about that world, and has become only a tribute to the geometer's cleverness. The only thing that the geometer needs is multiplicity, whereas the only thing the theologian needs is unity. Of unity, however vague, however tenuous, I see no evidence in modern science considered as a metaphysic. But modern science considered as common sense remains triumphant, indeed, more triumphant than ever before.

In view of this state of affairs, it is necessary to make

a sharp distinction between metaphysical beliefs and practical beliefs in regard to the conduct of life. In metaphysics my creed is short and simple. I think that the external world may be an illusion, but if it exists, it consists of events, short, small and haphazard. Order, unity, and continuity are human inventions just as truly as are catalogues and encyclopædias. But human inventions can, within limits, be made to prevail in our human world, and in the conduct of our daily life we may with advantage forget the realm of chaos and old night by which we are perhaps surrounded.

The ultimate metaphysical doubts which we have been considering have no bearing whatever upon the practical uses of science. If a Mendelian develops a variety of wheat which is immune from diseases that are destructive to the older varieties; if a physiologist makes a discovery about vitamins; if a chemist makes a discovery about the synthetic production of nitrates, the importance and usefulness of their work is quite independent of the question whether an atom consists of a miniature solar system, or a wave of probability, or an infinite rectangle of integers. When I speak of the importance of scientific method in regard to the conduct of human life, I am thinking of scientific method in its mundane forms. Not that I would undervalue science as a metaphysic, but the value of science as metaphysic belongs in another sphere. It belongs with religion and art and love, with the pursuit of the beatific vision, with the Promethean madness that leads the greatest men to strive to become gods. Perhaps the only ultimate value of human life is to be found in this Promethean madness. But it is a value that is religious, not political, or even moral.

It is this *quasi* religious aspect of the value of science which appears to be succumbing to the assaults of scepticism. Until quite recently men of science have felt themselves the high-priests of a noble cult, namely, the cult of truth; not truth as the religious sects understand it, i. e., as the battleground of a collection of dogmatists, but truth as a quest, a vision faintly appearing and again vanishing, a hoped-for sun to meet the Heraclitean fire in the soul. It is because science was so conceived, that men of science were willing to suffer privations and persecutions, and to be execrated as enemies of established creeds. All this is fading into the past; the modern man of science knows that he is respected, and feels that he does not deserve respect. He approaches the established order apologetically. "My predecessors," he says in effect, "may have said harsh things about you because they were arrogant, and imagined that they possessed some knowledge. I am more humble, and do not claim to know anything that can controvert your dogmas." In return, the established order showers knighthoods and fortunes upon the men of science, who become more and more determined supporters of the injustice and obscurantism upon which our social system is based. In the newer sciences, such as psychology, this has not yet happened; there the old ardour still persists, and the old persecutions continue. Homer Lane, for example, who was at once a sage and a saint, was deported by the British Police as an "undesirable alien." But these newer sciences have not yet been touched by the cold breath of scepticism, which has destroyed the life of physics and astronomy.

The trouble is an intellectual one; indeed, its solution, if there is one, is to be sought in logic. For my part, I have no solution to offer; our age is one which increasingly substitutes power for the older ideals, and this is happening in science as elsewhere. While science as the pursuit of power becomes increasingly triumphant, science as the pursuit of truth is being killed by a scepticism which the skill of the men of science has generated. That this is a misfortune is undeniable, but I cannot admit that the substitution of superstition for scepticism advocated by many of our leading men of science would be an improvement. Scepticism may be painful, and may be barren, but at least it is honest and an outcome of the quest for truth. Perhaps it is a temporary phase, but no real escape is possible by returning to the discarded beliefs of a stupider age.

CHAPTER V

Science and Religion

In recent times, the bulk of eminent physicists and a number of eminent biologists have made pronouncements stating that recent advances in science have disproved the older materialism, and have tended to re-establish the truths of religion. The statements of the scientists have as a rule been somewhat tentative and indefinite, but the theologians have seized upon them and extended them, while the newspapers in turn have reported the more sensational accounts of the theologians, so that the general public has derived the impression that physics confirms practically the whole of the Book of Genesis. I do not myself think that the moral to be drawn from modern science is at all what the general public has thus been led to suppose. In the first place, the men of science have not said nearly as much as they are thought to have said, and in the second place what they have said in the way of support for traditional religious beliefs has been said by them not in their cautious, scientific capacity, but rather in their capacity of good citizens, anxious to defend virtue and property. The War, and the Russian Revolution, have made all timid men conservative, and professors are usually temperamentally timid. Such considerations, however, are beside the point. Let us examine what science really has to say.

(1) *Free Will.*—Until very recent times theology, while in its Catholic form it admitted free will in human beings, showed an affection for natural law in the universe, tempered only by belief in occasional miracles. In the eighteenth century, under the influence of Newton, the alliance between theology and natural law became very close. It was held that God had created the world in accordance with a Plan, and that natural laws were the embodiment of this Plan. Until the nineteenth century theology remained hard and intellectual and definite. In order to meet the assaults of atheistic reason, however, it has, during the last hundred years, aimed more and more at appealing to sentiment. It has tried to catch men in their intellectually relaxed moods; and from having been a strait-jacket it has become a dressing-gown. In our day, only the fundamentalists and a few of the more learned Catholic theologians maintain the old respectable intellectual tradition. All the other religious apologists are engaged in blunting the edge of logic, appealing to the heart instead of the head, maintaining that our feelings can demonstrate the falsity of a conclusion to which our reason has been driven. As Lord Tennyson nobly says:

> *And like a man in wrath the heart*
> *Stood up and answered "I have felt."*

In our day the heart has feelings about atoms, about the respiratory system, about the growth of sea-urchins and other such topics, concerning which, but for science, it would remain indifferent.

One of the most remarkable developments in religious apologetics in recent times is the attempt to rescue free will in man by means of ignorance as to the behaviour of atoms. The older laws of mechanics which governed the movements of bodies large enough to be seen remain true to a very close approximation as regards such bodies, but are found to be not applicable to single atoms, still less to single electrons and protons. It is not yet known with any certainty whether there are laws governing the behaviour of single atoms in all respects, or whether the behaviour of such atoms is in part random. It is thought possible that the laws governing the behaviour of large bodies may be merely statistical laws, expressing the average result of a large number of random motions. Some, such as the second law of thermodynamics, are known to be statistical laws, and it is possible that others may be. In the atom there are various possible states which do not merge continuously into each other, but are separated by small finite gaps. An atom may hop from one of these states to another, and there are various different hops that it may make. At present no laws are known to decide which of the possible hops will take place on any given occasion, and it is suggested that the atom is not subject to laws at all in this respect, but has what might be called, by analogy, "free will." Eddington, in his book on the *Nature of the Physical World,* has made great play with this possibility (p. 311 ff.). He thinks, apparently, that the mind can decide the atoms in the brain to make one or another of the possible transitions at a given moment, and thus, by means of some kind of trigger action, produce large-scale results in accordance with its volition. The volition itself, he thinks, is uncaused. If he is right, the course of the physical world, even where fairly large masses are concerned, is not completely predetermined by physical laws, but is liable to be altered by the uncaused volitions of human beings.

Before examining this position I should like to say a few words about what is called "the Principle of Indeterminacy." This principle was introduced into physics in 1927 by Heisenberg, and has been seized on by clergymen—chiefly, I think, on account of its name—as something capable of giving them an escape from thraldom to mathematical laws. It is, to my mind, somewhat surprising that Eddington should countenance this use of the principle (see page 306). The Principle of Indeterminacy states that it is impossible to determine with precision both the position and the momentum of a particle; there will be a margin of error in each, and the product of the two errors is constant. That is to say, the more accurately we determine the one, the less accurately we shall be determining the other, and *vice versa.* The margin of error involved is, of course, very small. I am surprised, I repeat, that Eddington should have appealed to this principle in connexion with the question of free will, for the principle does nothing whatever to show that the course of nature is not determined. It shows merely that the old space-time apparatus is not quite adequate to the needs of modern physics, which, in any case, is known on other grounds. Space and time were invented by the Greeks, and served their purpose admirably until the present century. Einstein replaced them by a kind of centaur which he called "space-time," and this did well enough for a couple of decades, but modern quantum mechanics has made it evident that a more fundamental reconstruction is necessary. The Principle of Indeterminacy is merely an illustration of this necessity, not of the failure of physical laws to determine the course of nature.

As J. E. Turner has pointed out (*Nature*, December 27, 1930), "The use to which the Principle of Indeterminacy has been put is largely due to an ambiguity in the word 'determined.'" In one sense a quantity is determined when it is measured, in the other sense an event is determined when it is caused. The Principle of Indeterminacy has to do with measurement, not with causation. The velocity and position of a particle are declared by the Principle to be undetermined in the sense that they cannot be accurately measured. This is a physical fact causally connected with the fact that the measuring is a physical process which has a physical effect upon what is measured. There is nothing whatever in the Principle of Indeterminacy to show that any physical event is uncaused. As Turner says: "Every argument that, since some change cannot be 'determined' in the sense of 'ascertained,' it is therefore not 'determined' in the absolutely different sense of 'caused,' is a fallacy of equivocation."

Returning now to the atom and its supposed free will, it should be observed that it is not known that the behaviour of the atom is capricious. It is false to say the behaviour of the atom is known to be capricious, and it is also false to say the behaviour is known to be not capricious. Science has quite recently discovered that the atom is not subject to the laws of the older physics, and some physicists have somewhat rashly jumped to the conclusion that the atom is not subject to laws at all. Eddington's argument about the effect of the mind on the brain inevitably reminds one of Descartes's argument on the same subject. Descartes knew of the conservation of *vis viva*, but not of the conservation of momentum. He therefore thought that the mind could alter the direction of the motion of the animal spirits, though not its amount. When, shortly after the publication of his theory, the conservation of momentum was discovered, Descartes's view had to be abandoned. Eddington's view, similarly, is at the mercy of the experimental physicists, who may at any moment discover laws regulating the behaviour of individual atoms. It is very rash to erect a theological superstructure upon a piece of ignorance which may be only momentary. And the effects of this procedure, so far as it has any, are necessarily bad, since they make men hope that new discoveries will not be made.

There is, moreover, a purely empirical objection to the belief in free will. Wherever it has been possible to sub-

ject the behaviour of animals or of human beings to careful scientific observation, it has been found, as in Pavlov's
experiments, that scientific laws are just as discoverable as
in any other sphere. It is true that we cannot predict
human actions with any completeness, but this is quite
sufficiently accounted for by the complication of the mechanism, and by no means demands the hypothesis of complete lawlessness, which is found to be false wherever
it can be carefully tested.

Those who desire caprice in the physical world seem
to me to have failed to realize what this would involve.
All inference in regard to the course of nature is causal,
and if nature is not subject to causal laws all such inference
must fail. We cannot, in that case, know anything outside
of our personal experience; indeed, strictly speaking, we
can only know our experience in the present moment, since
all memory depends upon causal laws. If we cannot infer
the existence of other people, or even of our own past,
how much less can we infer God, or anything else that the
theologians desire. The principle of causality may be true
or may be false, but the person who finds the hypothesis
of its falsity cheering is failing to realize the implications
of his own theory. He usually retains unchallenged all
those causal laws which he finds convenient, as, for example, that his food will nourish him and that his bank
will honour his cheques so long as his account is in funds,
while rejecting all those that he finds inconvenient. This,
however, is altogether too *naïve* a procedure.

There is, in fact, no good reason whatever for supposing that the behaviour of atoms is not subject to law. It is only quite recently that experimental methods have been able to throw any light on the behaviour of individual atoms, and it is no wonder if the laws of this behaviour have not yet been discovered. To prove that a given set of phenomena is not subject to laws is essentially and theoretically impossible. All that can be affirmed is that the laws, if any, have not yet been discovered. We may say, if we choose, that the men who have been investigating the atom are so clever that they must have discovered the laws if there were any. I do not think, however, that this is a sufficiently solid premise upon which to base a theory of the universe.

(2) *God as Mathematician.*—Eddington deduces religion from the fact that atoms do not obey the laws of mathematics. Jeans deduces it from the fact that they do. Both these arguments have been accepted with equal enthusiasm by the theologians, who hold, apparently, that the demand for consistency belongs to the cold reason and must not interfere with our deeper religious feelings.

We have examined Eddington's argument from the way that atoms jump. Let us now examine Jeans's argument from the way that stars cool. Jeans's God is Platonic. He is not, we are told, a biologist or an engineer, but a pure mathematician (*The Mysterious Universe*, p. 134). I confess to a preference for this type of God rather than the one that is conceived after the analogy of big business; but that, no doubt, is because I prefer thinking to doing. This suggests a treatise dealing with the influence of muscular tone upon theology. The man whose muscles are taut believes in a God of action, while the man whose muscles are relaxed believes in a God of thought and contemplation. Jeans, confident no doubt in his own theistic arguments, is not very complimentary to those of the evolutionists. His book on the Mysterious Universe begins with a biography of the sun, one might almost say an epitaph. It seems that not more than one star in about one hundred thousand has planets, but that some two thousand million years ago the sun had the good fortune to have a fruitful meeting with another star, which led to the existing planetary offspring. The stars that do not have planets cannot give rise to life, so that life must be a very rare phenomenon in the universe. "It seems incredible," says Jeans, "that the universe can have been designed primarily to produce life like our own: had it been so, surely we might have expected to find a better proportion between the magnitude of the mechanism and the amount of the product." And even in this rare corner of the universe the possibility of life exists only during an interlude between weather that is too hot and weather that is too cold. "It is a tragedy of our race that it is probably destined to die of cold, while the greater part of the substance of the universe still remains too hot for life to obtain a footing." Theologians who argue as if human life were the purpose of creation seem to be as faulty in their astronomy as they are excessive in their estimation of themselves and their fellow-creatures. I shall not attempt to summarize Jeans's admirable chapters on modern physics, matter and radiation, and relativity and the ether; they are already as brief as possible, and no summary can do them justice. I will, however, quote Jeans's own summary in order to whet the reader's appetite.

"To sum up, a soap-bubble with irregularities and corrugations on its surface is perhaps the best representation, in terms of simple and familiar materials, of the new universe revealed to us by the theory of relativity. The universe is not the interior of the soap-bubble but its surface, and we must always remember that, while the surface of the soap-bubble has only two dimensions, the universe-bubble has four—three dimensions of space and one of time. And the substance out of which this bubble is blown, the soap-film, is empty space welded on to empty time."

The last chapter of the book is concerned to argue that this soap-bubble has been blown by a mathematical Deity because of His interest in its mathematical properties. This part has pleased the theologians. Theologians have grown grateful for small mercies, and they do not much care what sort of God the man of science gives them so long as he gives them one at all. Jeans's God, like Plato's, is one who has a passion for doing sums, but being a pure mathematician, is quite indifferent as to what the sums are about. By prefacing his argument by a lot of difficult and recent physics, the eminent author manages to give it an air of profundity which it would not otherwise possess. In essence the argument is as follows: since two apples and two apples together make four apples, it follows that the

Creator must have known that two and two are four. It might be objected that, since one man and one woman together sometimes make three, the Creator was not yet quite as well versed in sums as one could wish. To speak seriously: Jeans reverts explicitly to the theory of Bishop Berkeley, according to which the only things that exist are thoughts, and the quasi-permanence which we observe in the external world is due to the fact that God keeps on thinking about things for quite a long time. Material objects, for example, do not cease to exist when no human being is looking at them, because God is looking at them all the time, or rather because they are thoughts in His mind at all times. The universe, he says, "can best be pictured, although still very imperfectly and inadequately, as consisting of pure thought, the thought of what, for want of a wider word, we must describe as a mathematical thinker." A little later we are told that the laws governing God's thoughts are those which govern the phenomena of our waking hours, but not apparently of our dreams.

The argument is, of course, not set out with the formal precision which Jeans would demand in a subject not involving his emotions. Apart from all detail, he has been guilty of a fundamental fallacy in confusing the realms of pure and applied mathematics. Pure mathematics at no point depends upon observation; it is concerned with symbols, and with proving that different collections of symbols have the same meaning. It is because of this symbolic character that it can be studied without the help of experiment. Physics, on the contrary, however mathematical it may become, depends throughout on observation and experiment, that is to say, ultimately upon sense perception. The mathematician provides all kinds of mathematics, but only some of what he provides is useful to the physicist. And what the physicist asserts when he uses mathematics is something totally different from what the pure mathematician asserts. The physicist asserts that the mathematical symbols which he is employing can be used for the interpretation, colligation, and prediction of sense impressions. However abstract his work may become, it never loses its relation to experience. It is found that mathematical formulae can express certain laws governing the world that we observe. Jeans argues that the world must have been created by a mathematician for the pleasure of seeing these laws in operation. If he had ever attempted to set out this argument formally, I cannot doubt that he would have seen how fallacious it is. To begin with, it seems probable that any world, no matter what, could be brought by a mathematician of sufficient skill within the scope of general laws. If this be so, the mathematical character of modern physics is not a fact about the world, but merely a tribute to the skill of the physicist. In the second place, if God were as pure a pure mathematician as His knightly champion supposes, He would have no wish to give a gross external existence to His thoughts. The desire to trace curves and make geometrical models belongs to the schoolboy stage, and would be considered *infra dig* by a professor. Nevertheless it is this desire that Jeans imputes to his Maker. The world, he tells us, consists of thoughts; of these there are, it would seem, three grades: the thoughts of God, the thoughts of men when they are awake, and the thoughts of men when they are asleep and have bad dreams. One does not quite see what the two latter kinds of thought add to the perfection of the universe, since clearly God's thoughts are the best, and one does not quite see what can have been gained by creating so much muddle-headedness. I once knew an extremely learned and orthodox theologian who told me that as the result of long study he had come to understand everything except why God created the world. I commend this puzzle to the attention of Jeans, and I hope that he will comfort the theologians by dealing with it at no distant date.

(3) *God as Creator.*——One of the most serious difficulties confronting science at the present time is the difficulty derived from the fact that the universe appears to be running down. There are, for example, radio-active elements in the world. These are perpetually disintegrating into less complex elements, and no process by which they can be built up is known. This, however, is not the most important or difficult respect in which the world is running down. Although we do not know of any natural process by which complex elements are built up out of simpler ones, we can imagine such processes, and it is possible that they are taking place somewhere. But when we come to the second law of thermodynamics we encounter a more fundamental difficulty.

The second law of thermodynamics states, roughly speaking, that things left to themselves tend to get into a muddle and do not tidy themselves up again. It seems that once upon a time the universe was all tidy, with everything in its proper place, and that ever since then it has been growing more and more disorderly, until nothing but a drastic spring-cleaning can restore it to its pristine order. In its original form the second law of thermodynamics asserted something much less general: namely, that when there was a difference of temperature between two neighbouring bodies, the hotter one would cool and the colder one would get warmer until they reached an equal temperature. In this form the law states a fact familiar to everyone: if you hold up a red-hot poker, it will get cool while the surrounding air gets warm. But the law was soon seen to have a much more general meaning. The particles of very hot bodies are in very rapid motion, while those of cold bodies move more slowly. In the long run, when a number of swiftly moving particles and a number of slowly moving particles find themselves in the same region, the swift ones will bump into the slow ones until both sets acquire on the average equal velocities. A similar truth applies to all forms of energy. Whenever there is a great deal of energy in one region and very little in a neighbouring region, energy tends to travel from the one region to the other, until equality is established. This whole process may be described as a tendency towards democracy. It will be seen that this is an irreversible process, and that in the past energy must have been more unevenly distributed than it is now. In view of the fact that the material universe is now considered to be finite, and to consist of some definite though unknown number of electrons and protons, there is a theoretical limit to the possible heaping-up of energy in some places as opposed to others. As we trace the course of the world backwards in time, we arrive after some finite number of years (rather more than four thousand and four, however), at a state of the world which could not have been preceded by any other, if the second law of thermodynamics was then valid. This initial state of the world would be that in which energy was distributed as unevenly as possible. As Eddington says: [1]

The difficulty of an infinite past is appalling. It is inconceivable that we are the heirs of an infinite time of preparation; it is not less inconceivable that there was once a moment with no moment preceding it.

This dilemma of the beginning of time would worry us more were it not shut out by another overwhelming difficulty lying between us and the infinite past. We have been studying the running-down of the universe; if our views are right, somewhere between the beginning of time and the present day we must place the winding up of the universe.

Travelling backwards into the past we find a world with more and more organization. If there is no barrier to stop us earlier we must reach a moment when the

[1] Eddington, *The Nature of the Physical World*, 1928, p. 83 ff.

energy of the world was wholly organized with none of
the random element in it. It is impossible to go back any
further under the present system of natural law. I do not
think the phrase "wholly organized" begs the question.
The organization we are concerned with is exactly defin-
able, and there is a limit at which it becomes perfect.
There is not an infinite series of states of higher and still
higher organization; nor, I think, is the limit one which
is ultimately approached more and more slowly. Complete organization does not tend to be more immune from
loss than incomplete organization.

There is no doubt that the scheme of physics as it has
stood for the last three-quarters of a century postulates a
date at which either the entities of the universe were created in a state of high organization, or pre-existing entities
were endowed with that organization which they have
been squandering ever since. Moreover, this organization
is admittedly the antithesis of chance. It is something
which could not occur fortuitously.

This has long been used as an argument against a too
aggressive materialism. It has been quoted as scientific
proof of the intervention of the Creator at a time not infinitely remote from to-day. But I am not advocating that
we draw any hasty conclusions from it. Scientists and
theologians alike must regard as somewhat crude the
naïve theological doctrine which (suitably disguised) is at
present to be found in every textbook of thermodynamics,
namely, that some billions of years ago God wound up
the material universe and has left it to chance ever since.

*This should be regarded as the working-hypothesis of
thermodynamics rather than its declaration of faith. It is
one of those conclusions from which we can see no logical
escape—only it suffers from the drawback that it is incredible. As a scientist I simply do not believe that the
present order of things started off with a bang; unscien-
tifically I feel equally unwilling to accept the implied
discontinuity in the Divine nature. But I can make no suggestion to evade the deadlock.*

It will be seen that Eddington, in this passage, does
not infer a definite act of creation by a Creator. His only
reason for not doing so is that he does not like the idea.
The scientific argument leading to the conclusion which
he rejects is much stronger than the argument in favour
of free will, since that is based upon ignorance, whereas
the one we are now considering is based upon knowledge.
This illustrates the fact that the theological conclusions
drawn by scientists from their science are only such as
please them, and not such as their appetite for orthodoxy
is insufficient to swallow, although the argument would
warrant them. We must, I think, admit that there is far
more to be said for the view that the universe had a beginning in time at some not infinitely remote period, than
there is for any of the other theological conclusions which
scientists have recently been urging us to admit. The
argument does not have demonstrative certainty. The
second law of thermodynamics may not hold in all times
and places, or we may be mistaken in thinking the uni-

verse spatially finite; but as arguments of this nature go, it is a good one, and I think we ought provisionally to accept the hypothesis that the world had a beginning at some definite, though unknown, date.

Are we to infer from this that the world was made by a Creator? Certainly not, if we are to adhere to the canons of valid scientific inference. There is no reason whatever why the universe should not have begun spontaneously, except that it seems odd that it should do so; but there is no law of nature to the effect that things which seem odd to us must not happen. To infer a Creator is to infer a cause, and causal inferences are only admissible in science when they proceed from observed causal laws. Creation out of nothing is an occurrence which has not been observed. There is, therefore, no better reason to suppose that the world was caused by a Creator than to suppose that it was uncaused; either equally contradicts the causal laws that we can observe.

Nor is there, so far as I can see, any particular comfort to be derived from the hypothesis that the world was made by a Creator. Whether it was, or whether it was not, it is what it is. If somebody tried to sell you a bottle of very nasty wine, you would not like it any better for being told that it had been made in a laboratory and not from the juice of the grape. In like manner, I see no comfort to be derived from the supposition that this very unpleasing universe was manufactured of set purpose.

Some people—among whom, however, Eddington is not included—derive comfort from the thought that if

God made the world, He may wind it up again when it has completely run down. For my part, I do not see how an unpleasant process can be made less so by the reflection that it is to be indefinitely repeated. No doubt, however, that is because I am lacking in religious feeling.

The purely intellectual argument on this point may be put in a nutshell: is the Creator amenable to the laws of physics or is He not? If He is not, He cannot be inferred from physical phenomena, since no physical causal law can lead to Him; if He is, we shall have to apply the second law of thermodynamics to Him and suppose that He also had to be created at some remote period. But in that case He has lost His *raison d'être*. It is curious that not only the physicists, but even the theologians, seem to find something new in the arguments from modern physics. Physicists, perhaps, can scarcely be expected to know the history of theology, but the theologians ought to be aware that the modern arguments have all had their counterparts at earlier times. Eddington's argument about free will and the brain is, as we saw, closely parallel to Descartes's. Jeans's argument is a compound of Plato and Berkeley, and has no more warrant in physics than it had at the time of either of these philosophers. The argument that the world must have had a beginning in time is set forth with great clearness by Kant, who, however, supplements it by an equally powerful argument to prove that the world had no beginning in time. Our age has been rendered conceited by the multitude of new discoveries and inventions, but in the realm of philosophy it is much less in advance of the past than it imagines itself to be.

We hear a great deal nowadays about the old-fashioned materialism, and its refutation by modern physics. As a matter of fact, there has been a change in the technique of physics. In old days, whatever philosophers might say, physics proceeded technically on the assumption that matter consisted of hard little lumps. Now it no longer does so. But few philosophers ever believed in the hard little lumps at any date later than that of Democritus. Berkeley and Hume certainly did not; no more did Leibniz, Kant and Hegel. Mach, himself a physicist, taught a completely different doctrine, and every scientist with even a tincture of philosophy was ready to admit that the hard little lumps were no more than a technical device. In that sense materialism is dead, but in another and more important sense it is more alive than it ever was. The important question is not whether matter consists of hard little lumps or of something else, but whether the course of nature is determined by the laws of physics. The progress of biology, physiology, and psychology has made it more probable than it ever was before that all natural phenomena are governed by the laws of physics; and this is the really important point. To prove this point, however, we must consider some of the dicta of those who deal with the sciences of life.

(4) *Evolutionary Theology.*—Evolution, when it was new, was regarded as hostile to religion, and is still so considered by fundamentalists. But a whole school of

apologists has grown up who see in evolution evidence of a Divine Plan slowly unfolding through the ages. Some place this Plan in the mind of a Creator, while others regard it as immanent in the obscure strivings of living organisms. In the one view we fulfil God's purposes; in the other we fulfil our own, though these are better than we know. Like most controversial questions, the question of the purposiveness of evolution has become entangled in a mass of detail. When, long ago, Huxley and Mr. Gladstone debated the truth of the Christian religion in the pages of the *Nineteenth Century*, this great issue was found to turn upon the question whether the Gadarene swine had belonged to a Jew or a Gentile, since in the latter case, but not in the former, their destruction involved an unwarrantable interference with private property. Similarly the question of purpose in evolution becomes entangled in the habits of the amophila, the behaviour of sea-urchins when turned upside-down, and the aquatic or terrestrial habits of the axolotl. But such questions, grave as they are, we may leave to specialists.

In passing from physics to biology one is conscious of a transition from the cosmic to the parochial. In physics and astronomy we are dealing with the universe at large, and not only with that corner of it in which we happen to live, nor with those aspects of it which we happen to exemplify. From a cosmic point of view, life is a very unimportant phenomenon: very few stars have planets; very few planets can support life. Life, even on the earth, belongs to only a very small proportion of the matter close to the earth's surface. During the greater part of the past existence of the earth, it was too hot to support life; during the greater part of its future existence, it will be too cold. It is by no means impossible that there is, at this moment, no life anywhere in the universe except on the earth; but even if, taking a very liberal estimate, we suppose that there are scattered through space some hundred thousand other planets on which life exists, it must still be admitted that living matter makes rather a poor show if considered as the purpose of the whole creation. There are some old gentlemen who are fond of prosy anecdotes leading at last to a "point"; imagine an anecdote longer than any you have ever heard, and the "point" shorter, and you will have a fair picture of the activities of the Creator according to the biologists. Moreover, the "point" of the anecdote, even when it is reached, appears hardly worthy of so long a preface. I am willing to admit that there is merit in the tail of the fox, the song of the thrush, or the horns of the ibex. But it is not to these things that the evolutionary theologian points with pride: it is to the soul of man. Unfortûnately, there is no impartial arbiter to decide on the merits of the human race; but for my part, when I consider their poison gases, their researches into bacteriological warfare, their meannesses, cruelties and oppressions, I find them, considered as the crowning gem of the creation, somewhat lacking in lustre. But let that pass.

Is there anything in the process of evolution that demands the hypothesis of a purpose, whether immanent or transcendent? This is the crucial question. For one who is not a biologist it is difficult to speak otherwise than with hesitation on this question. I am, however, entirely unconvinced by the arguments in favour of purpose that I have seen.

The behaviour of animals and plants is on the whole such as to lead to certain results, which the observing biologist interprets as the purpose of the behaviour. In the case of plants, at any rate, he is generally willing to concede that this purpose is not consciously entertained by the organism; but that is all the better if he wishes to prove that it is the purpose of a Creator. I am, however, quite unable to see why an intelligent Creator should have the purposes which we must attribute to Him if He has really designed all that happens in the world of organic life. Nor does the progress of scientific investigation afford any evidence that the behaviour of living matter is governed by anything other than laws of physics and chemistry. Take, for example, the process of digestion. The first step in this process is the seizing of food. This has been carefully studied in many animals, more particularly in chickens. New-born chickens have a reflex which causes them to peck at any object having more or less the shape and size of edible grains. After some experience this unconditioned reflex becomes transformed into a conditioned reflex, exactly after the manner studied by Pavlov. The same thing may be observed in babies: they suck not only their mothers' breasts, but everything physically capable of being sucked; they endeavour to extract food out of shoulders and hands and arms. It is only after months of experience that they learn to confine their efforts after nourishment to the breast. Sucking in infants is at first an unconditioned reflex, and by no means an intelligent one. It depends for its success upon the intelligence of the mother. Chewing and swallowing are at first unconditioned reflexes, though through experience they become conditioned. The chemical processes which the food undergoes at various stages of digestion have been minutely studied, and none of them require the invocation of any peculiar vital principle.

Or take again reproduction, which, though not universal throughout the animal kingdom, is nevertheless one of its most interesting peculiarities. There is now nothing in this process that can rightly be called mysterious. I do not mean to say that it is all fully understood, but that mechanistic principles have explained enough of it to make it probable that, given time, they will explain the whole. Jacques Loeb, over twenty years ago, discovered means of fertilizing an ovum without the intervention of a spermatozoon. He sums up the results of his experiments and those of other investigators in the sentence: "We may, therefore, state that the complete imitation of the developmental effect of the spermatozoon by certain physico-chemical agencies has been accomplished."[1]

Take again the question of heredity, which is closely associated with that of reproduction. The present state of scientific knowledge in regard to this matter is set forth

[1] *The Mechanistic Conception of Life*, 1912, p. 11.

very ably by Professor Hogben in his book on *The Nature of Living Matter,* more particularly in the chapter on the atomistic view of parenthood. In this chapter the reader can learn all that a layman needs to know about the Mendelian theory, chromosomes, mutants, etc. I do not see how anybody can, in view of what is now known on these subjects, maintain that there is anything in the theory of heredity requiring us to bow down before a mystery. The experimental stage of embryology is still recent, yet it has achieved remarkable results: it has shown that the conception of an organism which had dominated biology is not nearly so rigid as had been supposed.

To graft the eye of one salamander tadpole on to the head of another individual is now a commonplace of experimental embryology. Five-legged and two-headed newts are now manufactured in the laboratory.[1]

But all this, the reader may say, is concerned only with the body; what are we to say concerning the mind? As to this, the question is not quite so simple. We may observe, to begin with, that the mental processes of animals are purely hypothetical, and that the scientific treatment of animals must confine itself to their behaviour and to their physical processes, since these alone are observable. I do not mean that we should deny that animals have minds; I mean merely that in so far as we are scientific we should say nothing about their minds one way or the

[1] Hogben, op. cit., p. 111.

other. As a matter of fact, the behaviour of their bodies appears to be causally self-contained, in the sense that its explanation does not, at any point, demand the intervention of some unobservable entity which we could call a mind. The theory of the conditioned reflex deals satisfactorily with all those cases in which it was formerly thought that a mental causation is essential for explaining the behaviour of the animal. When we come to human beings, we seem still able to explain the behaviour of human bodies on the assumption that there is no extraneous agent called mind acting upon them. But in the case of human beings this statement is much more questionable than in the case of other animals, both because the behaviour of human beings is more complex, and because we know, or think we know, through introspection, that we have minds. There is no doubt that we do know something about ourselves which is commonly expressed by saying that we have minds; but, as often happens, although we know something it is very difficult to say what we know. More particularly it is difficult to show that the causes of our bodily behaviour are not purely physical. It seems to introspection as though there were something called the will which causes those movements that we call voluntary. It is, however, quite possible that such movements have a complete chain of physical causes to which the will (whatever it may be) is a mere concomitant. Or perhaps, since the subject matter of physics is no longer matter in the old sense, it may be that what we call our thoughts are ingredients of the complexes with which physics has replaced the old conception of matter. The dualism of mind and matter is out-of-date: matter has become more like mind, and mind has become more like matter, than seemed possible at an earlier stage of science. One is led to suppose that what really exists is something intermediate between the billiard-balls of old-fashioned materialism and the soul of old-fashioned psychology.

There is here, however, an important distinction to be made. There is, on the one hand, the question as to the sort of stuff the world is made of, and on the other hand, the question as to its causal skeleton. Science has been from its inception, though at first not exclusively, a form of what may be called power-thought: that is to say, it has been concerned to understand what causes the processes we observe rather than to analyse the ingredients of which they are composed. The highly abstract scheme of physics gives, it would seem, the causal skeleton of the world, while leaving out all the colour and variety and individuality of the things that compose the world. In suggesting that the causal skeleton supplied by physics is, in theory, adequate to give the causal laws governing the behaviour of human bodies, we are not suggesting that this bare abstraction tells us anything about the contents of human minds, or for that matter about the actual constitution of what we regard as matter. The billiard-balls of old-fashioned materialism were far too concrete and sensible to be admitted into the framework of modern physics, but the same is true of our thoughts. The concrete variety of the actual world seems to be largely irrelevant when we are investigating these causal processes. Let us take an illustration. The principle of the lever is simple and easily understood. It depends only upon the relative positions of the fulcrum, force, and resistance. It may happen that the actual lever employed is covered with exquisite pictures by a painter of genius; although these may be of more importance from the emotional point of view than the mechanistic properties of the lever, they do not in any way affect those properties, and may be wholly omitted in an account of what the lever can do. So it is with the world. The world as we perceive it is full of a rich variety: some of it is beautiful, some of it is ugly; parts seem to us good, parts bad. But all this has nothing to do with the purely causal properties of things, and it is these properties with which science is concerned. I am not suggesting that if we knew these properties completely we should have a complete knowledge of the world, for its concrete variety is an equally legitimate object of knowledge. What I am saying is that science is that sort of knowledge which gives causal understanding, and that this sort of knowledge can in all likelihood be completed, even where living bodies are concerned, without taking account of anything but their physical and chemical properties. In saying this we are, of course, going beyond what can at present be said with any certainty, but the work that has been done in recent times in physiology, biochemistry, embryology, the mechanism of sensation,[1]

---

[1] See e. g. *The Basis of Sensation*, by E. D. Adrian, 1928.

and so on, irresistibly suggests the truth of our conclusion.

One of the best statements of the point of view of a religiously-minded biologist is to be found in Lloyd Morgan's *Emergent Evolution* (1923) and *Life, Mind and Spirit* (1926). Lloyd Morgan believes that there is a Divine Purpose underlying the course of evolution, more particularly of what he calls "emergent evolution." The definition of emergent evolution, if I understand it rightly, is as follows: it sometimes happens that a collection of objects arranged in a suitable pattern will have a new property which does not belong to the objects singly, and which cannot, so far as we can see, be deduced from their several properties together with the way in which they are arranged. He considers that there are examples of the same kind of thing even in the inorganic realm. The atom, the molecule, and the crystal will all have properties which, if I understand Lloyd Morgan aright, he regards as not deducible from the properties of their constituents. The same holds in a higher degree of living organisms, and most of all with those higher organisms which possess what are called minds. Our minds, he would say, are, it is true, associated with the physical organism, but are not deducible from the properties of that organism considered as an arrangement of atoms in space. "Emergent evolution," he says, "is from first to last a revelation and manifestation of that which I speak of as Divine Purpose." Again he says: "Some of us, and I for one, end with a concept of activity, under acknowledgment, as part and parcel of Divine Purpose." Sin, however, is not contributory to the manifestation of the Divine Purpose (p. 288).

It would be easier to deal with this view if any reasons were advanced in its favour, but so far as I have been able to discover from Professor Lloyd Morgan's pages, he considers that the doctrine is its own recommendation and does not need to be demonstrated by appeals to the mere understanding. I do not pretend to know whether Professor Lloyd Morgan's opinion is false. For aught I know to the contrary, there may be a Being of infinite power who chooses that children should die of meningitis, and older people of cancer; these things occur, and occur as the result of evolution. If, therefore, evolution embodies a Divine Plan, these occurrences must also have been planned. I have been informed that suffering is sent as a purification for sin, but I find it difficult to think that a child of four or five years old can be sunk in such black depths of iniquity as to deserve the punishment that befalls not a few of the children whom our optimistic divines might see any day, if they chose, suffering torments in children's hospitals. Again, I am told that though the child himself may not have sinned very deeply, he deserves to suffer on account of his parents' wickedness. I can only repeat that if this is the Divine sense of justice it differs from mine, and that I think mine superior. If indeed the world in which we live has been produced in accordance with a Plan, we shall have to reckon Nero a saint in comparison with the Author of that Plan. Fortunately, however, the evidence of Divine Purpose is non-existent; so at least one must infer from the fact that no evidence is adduced by those who believe in it. We are, therefore, spared the necessity for that attitude of impotent hatred which every brave and humane man would otherwise be called upon to adopt towards the Almighty Tyrant.

We have reviewed in this chapter a number of different apologies for religion on the part of eminent men of science. We have seen that Eddington and Jeans contradict each other, and that both contradict the biological theologians, but all agree that in the last resort science should abdicate before what is called the religious consciousness. This attitude is regarded by themselves and by their admirers as more optimistic than that of the uncompromising rationalist. It is, in fact, quite the opposite: it is the outcome of discouragement and loss of faith. Time was when religion was believed with whole-hearted fervour, when men went on crusades and burned each other at the stake because of the intensity of their convictions. After the wars of religion theology gradually lost this intense hold on men's minds. So far as anything has taken its place, its place has been taken by science. In the name of science we revolutionize industry, undermine family morals, enslave coloured races, and skilfully exterminate each other with poison gases. Some men of science do not altogether like these uses to which science is being put. In terror and dismay they shrink from the uncompromising pursuit of knowledge and try to find refuge in the superstitions of an earlier day. As Professor Hogben says:—

The apologetic attitude so prevalent in science to-day is not a logical outcome of the introduction of new concepts. It is based upon the hope of reinstating traditional beliefs with which science was at one time in open conflict. This hope is not a by-product of scientific discovery. It has its roots in the social temper of the period. For half a decade the nations of Europe abandoned the exercise of reason in their relations with one another. Intellectual detachment was disloyalty. Criticism of traditional belief was treason. Philosophers and men of science bowed to the inexorable decree of herd suggestion. Compromise to traditional belief became the hall-mark of good citizenship. Contemporary philosophy has yet to find a way out of the intellectual discouragement which is the heritage of a World War.[1]

It is not by going backward that we shall find an issue from our troubles. No slothful relapses into infantile fantasies will direct the new power which men have derived from science into the right channels; nor will philosophic scepticism as to the foundations arrest the course of scientific technique in the world of affairs. Men need a faith which is robust and real, not timid and half-hearted. Science is in its essence nothing but the systematic pursuit

[1] Hogben, op. cit., p. 28.

of knowledge, and knowledge, whatever ill-uses bad men may make of it, is in its essence good. To lose faith in knowledge is to lose faith in the best of man's capacities; and therefore I repeat unhesitatingly that the unyielding rationalist has a better faith and a more unbending optimism than any of the timid seekers after the childish comforts of a less adult age.

PART TWO

Scientific Technique

CHAPTER VI

Beginnings of Scientific Technique

No sharp line can be drawn between scientific technique and traditional arts and crafts. The essential characteristic of scientific technique is the utilization of natural forces in ways not evident to the totally uninstructed. A certain apparatus of desires is presupposed: men want food, offspring, clothing, housing, amusement, and glory. Uninstructed man can realize these things only very partially; man scientifically equipped can obtain much more of them. Compare, say, King Cyrus and a modern American billionaire. King Cyrus was, perhaps, the superior of the modern magnate in two respects; his clothes were grander, and his wives more numerous. At the same time, it is probable that his wives' clothes were not so grand as the clothes of the modern magnate's wife. It is part of the superiority of the modern magnate that he is not obliged to dress in glittering raiment in order to be known to be great; the newspapers see to this. I suppose not one hundredth as many people knew of Cyrus in his lifetime as know of a Hollywood star. This increased possibility of glory is due to scientific technique. In all the other objects of human desire which we enumerated just now, it is quite clear that modern technique has immensely increased the number of those who can enjoy a certain measure of satisfaction. The number of people who now own cars is greatly in excess of the number who had enough to eat one hundred and fifty years ago. By sanitation and hygiene the scientific nations have put an end to typhus and plague and a host of other diseases which still flourish in the East and formerly afflicted Western Europe. If one may judge by behaviour, one of the most ardent desires of the human race, or at any rate of its more energetic portions, has been until recently a mere increase of numbers. In this respect science has proved extraordinarily successful. Compare the number of people in Europe in the year 1700 with the number of European descent at the present day. The population of England in 1700 was about 5 million, and is now about 40 million. The population of other European countries, with the exception of France, has probably increased in about the same proportion. The population of European descent at the present day is about 725 millions. Other races, meanwhile, have increased very much less. It is true that in this respect a change is coming over the world. The most scientific races no longer increase much, and really rapid increases are now confined to countries in which the government is scientific while the population is unscientific. This, however, arises from quite recent causes which we shall not consider at present.

The earliest beginnings of scientific technique belong

to prehistoric times; nothing is known, for example, as to the origin of the use of fire, though the difficulty of procuring fire in early times is shown by the care with which sacred fires were tended in Rome and other early civilized communities. Agriculture also is prehistoric in origin, though perhaps it did not precede the dawn of history by any very long period. The domestication of animals is mainly prehistoric, but not wholly: according to some authorities, the horse burst upon Western Asia in the days of the Sumerians, and gave military victory to those who employed it in preference to the ass. In countries with a dry climate the beginning of writing practically coincides with the beginning of history, since early records survive in Egypt and Babylonia much longer than they would do in a less parched soil. The next great stage in scientific technique was the working of metals, which falls entirely within the historical epoch. It is no doubt because iron was a recent invention that in certain passages of the Bible its use is forbidden in the construction of altars. Roads, from the earliest period down to the fall of Napoleon, have been constructed chiefly for military reasons. They were essential to the coherence of large empires; they first became important for this purpose under the Persians, and were developed to their fullest extent by the Romans. The Middle Ages added gunpowder and the mariner's compass, and, at their very end, the invention of printing.

To one accustomed to the elaborate technique of modern life, all this may not seem to amount to very much, but it did in fact make the difference between primitive man and the highest grade of intellectual and artistic civilization. We are accustomed, in our own day, to protests against the empire of machinery and eloquent yearnings for a return to a simpler day. In all this there is nothing new. Lao-Tze, who preceded Confucius and lived (if he lived at all) in the sixth century B.C., is just as eloquent as Ruskin on the subject of the destruction of ancient beauty by modern mechanical inventions. Roads and bridges and boats filled him with horror because they were unnatural. He speaks of music as modern high-brows speak of the cinema. He finds the hurry of modern life fatal to the contemplative outlook. When he could bear it no longer he left China, and disappeared among the Western barbarians. He believed that men should live according to nature—a view which is continually recurring throughout the ages, though always with a different connotation. Rousseau also believed in the return to nature, but no longer objected to roads and bridges and boats. It was Courts and late hours and the sophisticated pleasures of the rich that roused his ire. The sort of man that seemed to him an unspoiled child of nature would have seemed to Lao-Tze incredibly different from those that he calls "the pure men of old." Lao-Tze objects to the taming of horses, and to the arts of the potter and carpenter; to Rousseau the carpenter would seem the very epitome of honest toil. "Return to nature" means, in practice, return to those conditions to which the writer in question was accustomed in his youth. Return to nature, if it were taken seriously, would involve the death by starvation of some 90 per cent. of the population of civilized countries. Industrialism as it exists at the present day undoubtedly has grave difficulties, but they are not to be cured by a return to the past, any more than were the difficulties from which China suffered in the time of Lao-Tze, or France in the time of Rousseau.

Science as knowledge advanced very rapidly throughout the whole of the seventeenth and eighteenth centuries, but it was not until near the end of the eighteenth century that it began to affect the technique of production. There was less change in methods of work from Ancient Egypt to 1750 than there has been from 1750 to the present day. Certain fundamental advances had been slowly acquired: speech, fire, writing, agriculture, the domestication of animals, the working of metals, gunpowder, printing, and the art of governing a large empire from a centre, though this last could not attain anything like its present perfection before the invention of the telegraph and steam locomotion. Each of these advances, because it came slowly, was fitted in, without too much difficulty, to the framework of traditional life, and men were at no point conscious of a revolution in their daily habits. Almost all the things that an adult man wished to speak about had been familiar to him as a child, and to his father and grandfather before him. This had, undoubtedly, certain good effects which have become lost through the rapid technical progress of modern times. The poet could speak of contemporary life in words that had become rich through long usage, and full of colour through the embedded emotions of past ages. Nowadays he must either ignore contemporary life, or fill his poems with words that are stark and harsh. It is possible, in poetry, to write a letter, but difficult to speak over the telephone; it is possible to listen to Lydian airs, but not to the radio; it is possible to ride like the wind upon a fiery steed, but difficult, in any known metre, to go much faster than the wind in an automobile. The poet may wish for wings to fly to his love, but feels rather foolish in doing so when he remembers that he could take an aeroplane.

The æsthetic effects of science have thus been on the whole unfortunate, not, I think, owing to any essential quality of science, but owing to the rapidly changing environment in which modern man lives. In other respects, however, the effects of science have been much more fortunate.

It is a curious fact that the doubts as to the ultimate metaphysical value of scientific knowledge have no bearing whatever upon its usefulness in relation to the technique of production. Scientific method is closely connected with the social virtue of impartiality. Piaget, in his book on *Judgment and Reasoning in the Child,* contends that the reasoning faculty is a product of the social sense. Every child, he says, begins with a dream of omnipotence, in which all facts are bent to his wishes. Gradually, through contact with others, he is forced to the realization that their wishes may be opposed to his, and that his wishes are not invariable arbiters of truth. Reasoning, according to Piaget, develops as a method of arriving at a social truth upon which all men can agree. This condition is, I think, largely valid, and emphasizes one great merit of the scientific method, namely, that it tends to avoid those intractable disputes which arise when private emotion is regarded as the test of truth. Piaget ignores another aspect of scientific method, namely, that it gives power over the environment and also power of adaptation to the environment. It may be, for example, an advantage to be able to predict the weather, and if one man is right on this point while all his companions are wrong, the advantage nevertheless remains with him, though a purely social definition of truth would compel us to regard him as in the wrong. It is success in this practical test of power over the environment, or adaptation to it, which has given science its prestige. The Chinese Emperors repeatedly refrained from persecuting the Jesuits because the latter were in the right as to the dates of eclipses when the Chinese astronomers were in the wrong. All modern life is built upon this practical success of science, at any rate where the inanimate world is concerned. It has had hitherto less success in direct applications to man, and it therefore still meets with opposition from traditional beliefs where man is concerned, but it cannot well be doubted that, if our civilization survives, man also will soon come to be viewed scientifically. This will have a great effect upon education and the criminal law, perhaps also on family life. Such developments, however, belong to the future.

The essential novelty about scientific technique is the utilization of natural forces in ways that are not obvious to untrained observation, but have been discovered by deliberate research. The use of steam, which was one of the earliest steps in modern technique, is on the border-line, since anybody can observe the force of steam in a kettle, as James Watt is traditionally supposed to have done. The use of electricity is far more definitely scientific. The use of water-power in an old-fashioned water-mill is pre-scientific, because the whole mechanism is patent to the untrained observer, but the modern use of water-power by means of turbines is scientific, since the process engendered is completely surprising to the person without scientific knowledge. Clearly the line between scientific and traditional technique is not a sharp one, and no one can say exactly where the one ends and the other begins. Primitive agriculturists used human bodies for manure, and imagined their beneficial effect to be magical. This stage was definitely pre-scientific. The use of natural manures, which succeeded it and has persisted down to our own day, is scientific if it is regulated by a careful study of organic chemistry, but unscientific if it proceeds by rule of thumb. The use of artificial nitrates, since it employs chemical processes only found after long search by skilful chemists, is definitely and unambiguously scientific.

The most essential characteristic of scientific technique is that it proceeds from experiment, not from tradition. The experimental habit of mind is a difficult one for most people to maintain; indeed, the science of one generation has already become the tradition of the next, and there are still wide fields, notably that of religion, into which the experimental spirit has hardly penetrated at all. Nevertheless it is this spirit which is characteristic of modern times as contrasted with all earlier ages, and it is because of this spirit that the power of man in relation to his environment has become, during the last hundred and fifty years, so immeasurably greater than it was in the civilization of the past.

CHAPTER VII

Technique in Inanimate Nature

THE greatest triumphs of applied science so far
have been in the realm of physics and chemistry.
When people think of scientific technique they
think primarily of machines. It seems probable that in
the near future science will achieve equal triumphs in
biological and physiological directions, and will ultimately
acquire as much power to change men's minds as it already
has power to deal with our inanimate environment. In
the present chapter, however, I shall not be concerned
with the biological applications of science, but with the
more familiar and hackneyed theme of its applications in
the realm of machinery.

Most machines, in the narrower sense of that word, do
not involve anything that deserves to be called science.
Machines were, in origin, merely a means of causing inanimate material to go through a series of regular movements which had hitherto been performed by the bodies,
and especially the fingers, of human beings. This is particularly obvious in the case of spinning and weaving.
Not very much science was involved in the invention of
railways, or in the early stages of steam-navigation. Men

were here utilizing forces that were by no means recondite in ways which, though they astonished, ought not to have been astonishing. When we come to electricity, however, the matter is otherwise. A practical electrician has to develop a new type of common sense, of which the man ignorant of electricity is totally devoid. This new type of common sense consists entirely of knowledge discovered by means of science. A man whose days have been passed in a simple rural existence knows the kind of thing that a mad bull is likely to do, but however old and sagacious he may become he will not know what an electric current is likely to do.

One of the purposes of industrial technique has always been to substitute other forms of power for the power of human muscles. Animals depend completely upon their own muscles for securing the satisfaction of their wants, and primitive man, one must suppose, shared this dependence. Gradually, as men acquired more knowledge, they became increasingly able to command sources of power which left their own muscles unfatigued. Some genius in some forgotten antiquity invented the wheel, and some other genius induced the ox and the horse to make the wheel go round. It must have been a much more difficult job to tame the ox and the horse than it has proved to tame electricity, but the difficulty was one of patience, not of intelligence. Electricity, like a djinn in the *Arabian Nights*, is a patient servant to anyone who knows the right formula: the discovery of the formula is difficult, but the rest is easy. In the case of the ox and the horse no great skill was required to see that their muscles could do more effectively the work that human muscles had previously done, but it must have been a long time before the ox and the horse became submissive to the will of their tamers. There are those who say that they were tamed because they were worshipped, and that the practical utilization of them came later, after the priests had completely domesticated them. This theory is inherently probable, since almost all great advances have sprung originally from disinterested motives. Scientific discoveries have been made for their own sake and not for their utilization, and a race of men without a disinterested love of knowledge would never have achieved our present scientific technique. Take, for example, the theory of electro-magnetic waves, upon which the use of wireless depends. Relevant scientific knowledge begins with Faraday, who first investigated experimentally the connexion of the intervening medium with electric phenomena. Faraday was no mathematician, but his results were reduced to mathematical form by Clerk-Maxwell, who discovered by means of purely theoretical constructions that light consists of electro-magnetic waves. The next stage in the proceedings was due to Hertz, who first artificially manufactured electro-magnetic waves. What remained to be done was merely to invent apparatus by which these waves could be produced with a commercial profit. This step, as everyone knows, was taken by Marconi. Faraday, Maxwell, and Hertz, so far as can be discovered, never for a moment considered the possibility of any practical application of their investigations. Indeed, until the investigations were almost completed it was impossible to foresee the uses to which they could be put.

Even in cases where the purpose throughout has been practical, the solution of one problem has very often resulted from the solution of another with which it had no apparent connexion. Take, for example, the problem of flying. This has, at all times, exercised men's imaginations. Leonardo da Vinci devoted far more time to it than he did to painting. But men were misled until our own day by the notion that they must find a mechanism analogous to the wings of birds. It was only the discovery of the petrol engine, and its development for the sake of motor-cars, that led to a solution of the problem of flying, and in the early stages of the petrol engine it did not occur to anyone that it would prove capable of this application.

One of the most difficult problems of modern technique is that of raw materials. Industry uses up, at a continually increasing rate, substances which have been stored throughout geological time in the earth's crust, and which are not being replaced in any usable form. One of the most flagrant instances is oil. The supply of oil in the world is limited, and the consumption of oil is continually and rapidly increasing. It will probably not be very long before the world's supply is practically exhausted—unless indeed the wars which will take place for its possession are sufficiently destructive to reduce the level of civilization to a point where oil will no longer be needed. We may, I suppose, assume, if our civilization has not suffered a cataclysm, that some substitute for oil will be discovered as oil becomes more expensive through rarity. But, as this example shows, industrial technique can never become static and traditional as agricultural technique did in former times. It will be perpetually necessary to invent new processes and to find new sources of power, owing to the extraordinary rapidity with which we are consuming our terrestrial capital. There are, of course, some practically inexhaustible sources of power, notably wind and water; the latter, however, even if fully utilized, would be very inadequate to the world's needs. The utilization of wind, owing to its irregularity, would require vast accumulators more free from leakage than any that can now be manufactured.

The dependence upon natural products which we have inherited from a simpler age is likely to grow less with the progress of chemistry. It is probable that in a very near future synthetic rubber will replace the rubber-tree, as artificial silk is already replacing natural silk. Artificial woods can already be manufactured, though this is not yet a commercial proposition. But the exhaustion of the world's forests, which is imminent owing to the growth of newspapers, will soon make it necessary to employ other materials than wood-pulp for the production of paper—unless indeed the habit of hearing the news on the wireless leads men to abandon the written word as the source of their daily sensation.

One of the scientific possibilities of the future which

may have great importance is the control of climate by
artificial means. There are those who say that if a break-
water some twenty miles long were constructed at a suitable point on the Eastern coast of Canada, it would completely transform the climate of Southeast Canada and
New England, since it would cause the cold current which
now flows along their shores to sink to the bottom of the
sea, leaving the surface to be replenished by warm water
from the South. I do not vouch for the truth of this idea,
but it serves to illustrate possibilities which may in future
be realized. To take another illustration: the greater part
of the land between latitudes 30° and 40° has been
gradually drying up and supports at present, in many
regions, a much smaller population than it did two thousand years ago. In Southern California irrigation has
transformed the desert into one of the most fertile regions
of the world. There is no known means of irrigating the
Sahara or the Gobi Desert, but perhaps the problem of
rendering these regions fertile will not, in the end, prove
beyond the resources of science.

Modern technique has given man a sense of power
which is rapidly altering his whole mentality. Until recent times, the physical environment was something which
had to be accepted and made the best of. If the rainfall
became insufficient to support life, the only alternatives
were death or migration. Those who were strong in war
adopted the latter, and those who were weak the former.
To the modern man his physical environment is merely
raw material, an opportunity for manipulation. It may be

that God made the world, but that is no reason why we should not make it over. This attitude, far more than any intellectual arguments, is proving inimical to traditional religion. Traditional religion embodied the idea of man's dependence upon God. This idea, while still nominally acknowledged, no longer has the hold on the imagination of the modern scientific industrialist that it had on the primitive peasant or fisherman, to whom droughts or storms might bring death. To the typical modern mind nothing is interesting on account of what it is, but only on account of what it may be made to become. The important characteristics of things from this point of view are not their intrinsic qualities, but their uses. Everything is an instrument. If you ask what it is an instrument to, the answer will be that it is an instrument for the making of instruments, which will in turn make still more powerful instruments, and so on *ad infinitum*. In psychological terms, this means that the love of power has thrust aside all the other impulses that make the complete human life. Love, parenthood, pleasure, and beauty are of less account to the modern industrialist than to the princely magnates of past times. Manipulation and exploitation are the ruling passions of the typical scientific industrialist. The average man may not share this narrow concentration, but for that very reason he fails to acquire a hold on the sources of power, and leaves the practical government of the world to the fanatics of mechanism. The power of producing changes in the world which is possessed by the leaders of big business in the present age far exceeds the power ever possessed by individuals in the past. They may not be as free to cut off heads as were Nero or Jenghiz Khan, but they can settle who shall starve and who shall become rich, they can divert the course of rivers, and decree the fall of governments. All history shows that great power is intoxicating. Fortunately, the modern holders of power are not yet quite aware how much they could do if they chose, but when this knowledge dawns upon them a new era in human tyranny is to be expected.

CHAPTER VIII

Technique in Biology

SCIENTIFIC technique has been applied by human beings to satisfy a number of diverse desires. At first it was applied mainly to the production of clothing and to the transport of goods and human beings. With the telegraph it acquired important functions in the rapid transmission of messages, making possible the modern newspaper and the centralization of government. A great deal of first-class scientific intelligence has found its chief effect in the increase of trivial amusement. The most fundamental of all human needs, namely, food, was at first not much influenced by the Industrial Revolution; the opening-up of the American Middle West by means of railways was the first great change in regard to food that was caused by scientific technique. Since that time Canada, the Argentine, and India have become important sources of grain for European countries. The mobility of cereals which we owe to railways and steamships has removed the menace of famine which hung over all mediæval countries, and which has, even in quite recent years, afflicted both Russia and China. This change, however, important as it is, has not been due to the application of science to agriculture. In recent times biological science has been found of growing importance in relation to the food supply. Economists used to teach that modern technique could only cheapen manufactured articles, while food was to increase steadily in price as population increased. It did not, until recently, appear probable that a revolution in food production as important as the revolution in the production of manufactured goods might be brought about by the application of science. Nowadays, however, this seems far from improbable.

There has not been, in relation to agriculture, any one resounding and revolutionary invention analogous to the introduction of steam, but a number of different lines of research have each contributed something towards a result which, in the aggregate, is likely to be very large.

Take, for example, the question of nitrogen in agriculture. Everybody knows that all living bodies, whether of plants or animals, contain a certain percentage of nitrogen. Animals obtain nitrogen only by eating plants or other animals. How do plants obtain nitrogen? This was for a long time a mystery; it seemed natural to suppose that they might obtain it from the air (more particularly from the small quantities of ammonia which it contains), but experiments proved that this was not the case. This conclusion having been arrived at, it remained to discover how plants obtained nitrogen from the soil. This problem was studied by two men, Lawes and Gilbert, who throughout a period of sixty years conducted a series of experiments at Rothamsted, near Harpenden. They found that the great majority of plants do not possess the power of fixing nitrogen. In the year 1886, however, Hellriegel and Wilfrath found that clover and other leguminous plants have a special part to play in the fixation of nitrogen. This was due to nodules in their roots, or rather not to the nodules themselves, but to certain species of bacteria which lived in the nodules. If the bacteria were absent, these plants were no better than others with regard to fixation of nitrogen; the bacteria, therefore, are the essential agents.

It may be said generally that bacteria alone, so far as is known at present, have the power, some to transform ammonia into nitrates, and others to utilize atmospheric nitrogen. Ammonia consists of nitrogen and hydrogen, while nitrates consist of nitrogen and oxygen. Certain bacteria in the soil possess the power of getting rid of the hydrogen in ammonia, and replacing it by oxygen. The nitrates which they thus produce are capable of nourishing ordinary plants. It is partly in this way, and partly by means of the bacteria that utilize atmospheric nitrogen, that nitrogen passes from the inanimate world into the life cycle.[1]

Until the exploitation of Chilean nitrates, this was the only way in which the nitrates required to support life came into being. The nitrates that were used as manure all had an organic origin. The nitrates to be found in Chile and elsewhere are limited in quantity, and if agriculture had to depend upon them alone it would soon be faced

[1] *The Materials of Life,* by T. R. Parsons, 1930, p. 263.

with a crisis through their becoming exhausted. Nowadays, however, nitrates are artificially manufactured from the nitrogen in the air—a source which is, for all practical purposes, inexhaustible. The amount of nitrate produced in this way is now greatly in excess of that obtained from all other sources. By means of nitrate fertilizers the food production in a given area can be greatly increased. It is calculated that one ton of nitrogen in the form of sulphate of ammonia or nitrate of soda will produce enough food for thirty-four people for one year.[1] It appears, as a result of this calculation, that $15 spent in producing nitrogen fertilizers will add as much to the world's supply of food as $125 spent in bringing new land under cultivation. It follows that, at the present time, the production of nitrogen fertilizers is, in general, more profitable in relation to the world's food supply than the opening up of new land by means of railways or irrigation. This example of the application of science to agriculture is interesting, because it involves both organic and inorganic chemistry, together with a careful study of the complete life cycle in plants and animals.

A very interesting field for scientific research has been opened up in connexion with the control of pests. Most pests are either insects or fungi, and in regard to both kinds much valuable knowledge has been acquired in recent years. The importance of such knowledge is very little realized by the general public, and is not appreciated by governments except when it can be connected with

[1] *Nature*, October 11, 1930.

nationalism. The popular imagination has, it is true, been struck by certain specially noteworthy instances. The control of malaria and yellow fever by preventing the mosquito from breeding has made it possible to render many formerly deadly regions habitable to white men, and in particular was necessary for the construction of the Panama Canal. The connexion of the bubonic plague with rats' fleas and of typhus with lice has also become part of the knowledge of educated people. But apart from such isolated examples few people except specialists and certain government officials realize the existence of a vast field of research, which is important in various directions, but especially in relation to the world's food supply.

As regards insect pests, some notion as to what has been done and is to be done may be derived from an article in *Nature* (January 10, 1931) called "Entomology and the British Empire." This gives an account of the work of the Third Imperial Entomological Conference and of the Imperial Institute (formerly Bureau) of Entomology. I wonder how many of my readers know that such bodies exist; yet it appears that on the average 10 per cent. of the agricultural produce of the world is destroyed each year by insects. As the above-mentioned article states: "It is estimated that in the Indian Empire, for example, the losses in 1921 due to crop and forest pests alone reached the huge total of $680,000,000, while the death-roll among the population due to insect-born diseases was stated to be about 1,600,000 persons annually. In Canada about $150,000,000 is lost every year through insect depradations among field and fruit crops and to forests. In South Africa one pest, the maize-stalk borer (*Busseola fusca*), incurred losses of about $13,750,000 in a single year."

There are two kinds of methods of controlling insect pests, namely, physico-chemical methods and biological methods. The former consist usually of fumigation. The latter, which are the more interesting scientifically, consist in the discovery of parasites which will prey on the destructive insects, on the principle expressed in the rhyme: "Big fleas have little fleas upon their backs to bite 'em; little fleas have smaller fleas, and so on *ad infinitum*." In general, in the regions where a pest is indigenous, some parasite exists which keeps its numbers down; but when the pest is accidentally introduced into a new country the parasite may be left behind, with the result that the pest effects an intensity of destruction quite out of proportion to what it can achieve at home. Modern improvements in transport have, of course, promoted the spread of noxious insects, and have therefore rendered the problem of their control more urgent.

Even when there is no question of transference to a new *habitat*, a great deal can be done, in many cases, by artificial encouragement of useful parasites. Let us take an example of a pest the danger of which is familiar to everyone who has ever grown tomatoes under glass: I mean the greenhouse white-fly. An account of the biological control of this pest is given by Mr. E. R. Speyer in *Nature*, December 27, 1930. An insect parasite on the white-fly, called *Encarsia formosa*, was discovered at Elstree in Hertfordshire in 1926, and has since then been carefully bred at the Cheshunt Experimental Station, whence it can be obtained by those who desire it. Throughout the county of Hertfordshire, where the area of cultivation under glass is about equal to that in the whole of the rest of Great Britain, the parasites that have escaped from Cheshunt have been sufficiently numerous to reduce the white-fly population to a small fraction of what it was six years ago.

Economic entomology is a subject of great importance, in which the United States is far ahead of the British Empire, though its potential usefulness in the latter is at least as great as in the former. Such problems as the extermination of the locust and the tse-tse fly (which is the cause of sleeping sickness) will probably be not beyond the resources of science in the near future.

Fungi are scarcely less harmful as pests than insects. The study of them in England is conducted mainly by the Imperial Mycological Institute at Kew, which is supported by the Empire Marketing Board. An interesting article on the work of this Institute appeared in *The Times*, February 2, 1931. One of the most familiar and harmful of fungus pests is the disease of wheat called rust. The Canadian Government catches the spores of this plant in aeroplanes, to discover how it is spread by the wind. The importance of the matter to Canada may be judged from the fact that in 1916, at the height of the war, black rust destroyed wheat to the value of about $175,000,000 in the three Prairie Provinces alone, and averages in Canada a destruction of about $25,000,000 annually. Potato blight, which is another kind of fungus, caused the Irish famine, and thence led England to adopt free trade and Boston to ban modern literature. This particular disease has now been brought under control, and England is about to abandon free trade. The effect of the fungus on Boston, however, appears to be more permanent.

A curious example of a point of contact between different techniques occurred in connexion with the construction of aeroplanes, in the wooden parts of which the sitka spruce, which grows in British Columbia, is largely employed. As to this, the above-mentioned article in *The Times* states:

A surprisingly large percentage of apparently unblemished timber was at one time found to break down. No sign of fungal infection could at first be seen; but examination at the Institute under a microscope revealed the minute tentacles of a fungus. A Canadian woman worker took up the problem, travelled through the British Columbian forests, and discovered the source of infection of the unfelled timber. Co-operative work between the Forest Products Research Laboratory at Prince's Risborough and its opposite number in Canada showed, further, that the disease was accentuated by the long voyage through the tropics via *the Panama Canal. The trouble has been largely eliminated by careful examination of trees before they are cut and by overland transport.*

These few examples may serve to show the economic importance of mycology, the science of fungi.

Another direction in which biological technique is likely to have great importance before long is scientific breeding. Artificial selection has been applied by man for ages to animals and plants under domestication, and has yielded remarkable results. No wild plant exists of the same species as wheat. The cow, having long been bred for her milk-producing qualities, has become very different from any wild animal that ever existed. The racehorse is a highly artificial product. But these results, remarkable as they are, have been produced by methods which can scarcely be called scientific. Nowadays, especially by means of the Mendelian principles of heredity, there is hope of breeding new varieties of animals and plants in a less haphazard manner. So far, however, what has been attempted in this way gives scarcely more than a suggestion of what may be rendered possible by new discoveries in regard to heredity and embryology.

The importance of animals in human life has greatly diminished since the Industrial Revolution. Abraham lived among his flocks and herds; Attila's armies travelled on horses. In the modern world, animals play a very small part as a source of power, and in particular have become quite subordinate as a means of transport. They are still used for food and clothing, but in regard to these also they will soon be largely superseded. The silkworm is threatened by artificial silk; real leather will soon be regarded as a luxury for the rich. As yet, wool is still used to make warm clothes, but it is likely that synthetic products will replace it before long. As for meat, it is not a necessary article of diet, and if population continues to increase we may assume that synthetic beef-steaks will be served everywhere except at the tables of millionaires. The cod may survive somewhat longer than the ox, for the sake of the vitamins in cod-liver oil. But already vitamin D can be generated in the human body by means of artificial sunlight, so that even the cod may not remain necessary very long. Animals have been good friends to man throughout his adolescence, after being dangerous enemies in his infancy. But now that man is becoming adult, the part played by animals in relation to man is ending, and their future will be mainly confined to Zoos. One cannot help regretting this, but it is part of the new ruthlessness of man intoxicated by scientific power.

The need for plants will survive longer than the need for animals, because they are as yet essential to the chemical processes upon which human life depends. The use of vegetable products for purposes other than food is not very difficult to dispense with. It is possible already to manufacture substances resembling wood in so far as its useful properties are concerned, though as yet the process of manufacture is more expensive than growing the timber. When it becomes cheaper, as it inevitably will, forests will lose their economic value. It is not probable that natural cotton will continue to be used in clothing, any more than natural silk. Synthetic rubber will soon replace natural rubber. Almost all such uses of vegetable products, it may be safely assumed, will cease to be important before another hundred years have passed.

Food is a more serious matter. It is said to be already possible to manufacture from the air products which can be eaten and digested, though there are two objections to them, namely, that they are nauseous and expensive. Both these objections may in time be overcome. The problem of producing synthetic food is purely chemical, and there is no reason to regard it as insoluble. No doubt natural foods will taste better, and rich men, at weddings and feasts, will provide real peas and beans, which will be mentioned by the newspapers with awe. But in the main food will be manufactured in vast chemical factories. The fields will fall out of cultivation, and agricultural labourers will be replaced by chemical experts. In such a world, no biological processes will be of interest to man except those that take place in himself. These will be so out of the picture that he will tend more and more to view himself also as a manufactured product, and to minimize the share of natural growth in the production of human beings. He will come to value only what is deliberately caused by human agency, not what results from nature's unaided handiwork. Men will acquire power to alter themselves, and will inevitably use this power. What they will make of the species I do not venture to predict.

CHAPTER IX

Technique in Physiology

A LIVING body, considered as a physico-chemical mechanism, has some very remarkable properties, which, so far, no machine of human construction can imitate. The physical parts of the mechanism, such as the heart's action in pumping the blood, and the working of muscles and bones, are less remarkable than the chemical portions, but have at any rate the merit of seldom going seriously out of order. The heart has to work day and night throughout the whole of a man's life —say, seventy years. Repairs, if any are needed, have to be effected while it is working. An ordinary healthy man is much less often ill than the best of motor-cars, in spite of the fact that his engine never gets a rest. The physics of the human body is excellent, but is less complex and interesting than its chemistry.

The most remarkable properties of a living body, as opposed to a lifeless one, are nourishment, growth, and predetermination. Nourishment consists in the fact that a living body, by means of various physical apparatus, enters into chemical contact with suitable foreign bodies, and subjects them to a laboratory treatment which transforms as much of them as possible into substances chemically similar to itself and ejects the useless residue. Growth consists in the fact that, by means of cell division and nourishment, the visible complexity of a living body can increase at the same time with its bulk. Predetermination, which is a property of both nourishment and growth, consists in the fact that nourishment is used to keep an adult body nearly unchanging in structure and chemical composition, while in the young growth reproduces, within narrow limits, the structure of the parents. As thus defined, predetermination embraces reproduction and heredity. It seems, at first sight, an almost mystical property of living matter, but science is gradually coming to understand it, though as yet far from completely.

Nourishment—the transformation of food into various parts of the body—is a process of quite amazing complexity. Some aspects of it, for example the operation of vitamins, remain obscure. But the essential characteristic of nourishment is comparatively simple. From the saliva onwards a series of chemical agents act upon our food, until it reaches the condition in which it is fit to enter the bloodstream, out of which the various parts of the body extract what they need, again by means of various chemical agencies.

Growth is seen in its most remarkable form in the newly fertilized ovum, which rapidly divides into two cells, then four, then eight, and so on, while continually increasing in size. Growth is capable of assuming morbid forms, for instance in cancer.

Predetermination is exhibited not only in heredity, but in the ordinary repairs to the wear and tear of the body. When hair and nails are cut, they grow again; when the skin is scratched, new skin forms; when the body has been wasted by illness, it reverts, with returning health, to very nearly what it was before. Within limits, a living body has the power of restoring itself to its previous structure when it has suffered some not too violent disturbance. Heredity is an example of the same power. There must be differences between human and simian spermatozoa corresponding to the differences between men and monkeys, though the microscope is not sufficiently powerful to reveal them. We must suppose that throughout the growth of the foetus a pre-existing complexity is becoming visible, since otherwise the fact of heredity is unintelligible. The development of the embryo is therefore, from the standpoint of logic, strictly analogous to the self-preservative quality of the adult body. And it is, of course, true only within similar limits.

Technique in physiology has hitherto chiefly taken the form of medicine in the widest sense, i. e., the prevention and cure of disease and death. What has been accomplished in this respect is obvious from mortality statistics. The changes in the death-rate in England and Wales since 1870 have been as follows:

1870 . . . . 22.9 per thousand
1929 . . . . 13.4 per thousand

In other civilized countries the changes have been similar. At the same time, owing to another form of technique in physiology, the birth-rate has been declining, as the following figures show:

> 1870 . . . . 35.3 *per thousand*
> 1929 . . . . 16.3 *per thousand*

There are many consequences of these figures. One is that there is ceasing to be any natural increase of population in civilized countries, and that there may before long be an actual diminution. The other is that there are fewer young people and more old people. Those who believe that the old are wiser than the young will expect good results from this change in the balance between age and youth. On the other hand it will be regretted by those who feel that, in our rapidly changing world, the old are less likely than the young to understand new forces, and more likely than the young to overestimate decaying forces that are losing their importance. This, however, may be counteracted by a prolongation of physiological youth.

Reproduction operated, until recently, as blindly as a natural force. This, at any rate, was the case among Europeans, though many savage and barbarous peoples employed various methods of artificial limitation of fertility. During the last fifty years reproduction among the white races has become increasingly deliberate instead of accidental. As yet, this fact has not produced the political and social consequences that it is bound to entail sooner or later; what these consequences are likely to be we will consider at a later stage.

Artificial prevention of impregnation is not the only change brought about by modern technique in this respect, though so far it has been the most important. It is also possible to cause impregnation artificially. So far, this process has not been much developed, but when it has been perfected it may be a source of very important changes in connexion with eugenics and the family.

If it should ever become possible to determine sex at will there would inevitably be an important readjustment of the relations between men and women. The first effect, one may surmise, would be a considerable excess of male births. This would, in the course of a generation, confer a scarcity value on women, and introduce overt or surreptitious polyandry. The respect for women would be enhanced by their rarity, with the result that female births would begin to preponderate. In the end, the State would probably have to regulate the matter by a bonus for the sex which was deficient at the moment. These successive oscillations and administrative measures would have bewildering effects upon emotions and morals.

It is probable that the most important application of physiological technique, in the long run, will be to embryology. Hitherto medicine and even biochemistry have aimed only at health, that is to say, at the perfect functioning of a body which had been produced by natural causes. The only method that has been suggested for improving the human stock has been that of eugenics. Heredity, where the higher animals and man are concerned, is as yet not subject to human control. A given embryo can develop into a healthy or a sickly individual, but if it is to be healthy it can be only one sort of individual, at any rate in so far as its heritable characteristics are concerned. Mutations occur, but they cannot be produced at will. This, however, is not likely to remain always the case. There has been much controversy as to the inheritance of acquired characters, and it seems clear that this does not occur in the form in which Lamarck believed. No change in an organism is inherited unless it affects the chromosomes, which are the bearers of hereditary characters; but a change which affects the chromosomes may be inherited.[1] When the larvæ of the fruit-fly are exposed, at an early stage, to the operation of X-rays, they develop into adults which differ noticeably from most ordinary fruit-flies. It may be that the changes produced by X-rays affect the chromosomes as well as the rest of the body, and that, if so, they can be inherited. Changes of temperature or of diet may possibly affect the chromosomes. Knowledge on these matters is still in its infancy. But since mutations occur, it is clear that there are agencies which alter the hereditary character of an organism. When these have been discovered it may be possible to apply them artificially in such a way as to produce some intended result. In that case, eugenics

[1] See Hogben, *The Nature of Living Matter*, p. 186.

will no longer be the only way of improving a breed.

So far, no experiments have been made to test the effect of X-rays on the human embryo. I imagine that such experiments would be illegal, in common with many others that might make valuable additions to our knowledge. Sooner or later, however, probably in Russia, such experiments will be made. If science continues to advance as fast as it has done recently, we may hope, before the end of the present century, to discover ways of beneficially influencing the human embryo, not only as regards those acquired characters which cannot be inherited because they do not affect the chromosomes, but also as regards the chromosomes themselves. It is likely that this result will only be achieved after a number of unsuccessful experiments leading to the birth of idiots or monstrosities. But would this be too high a price to pay for the discovery of a method by which, within one generation, the whole human race could be rendered intelligent? Perhaps by a suitable choice of chemicals to be injected into the uterus it may become possible to turn a child into a mathematician, a poet, a biologist, or even a politician, and to ensure that all his posterity shall do likewise unless prevented by counter-irritant chemicals. The sociological effect of such a possibility is a vast subject, which we will not consider at present. But it would be very rash to deny that some such possibility may exist in the near future.

While it is rather rash to make detailed prophecies, it is, I think, fairly clear that in future a human body, from the moment of conception, will not be regarded merely as something which must be left to grow in accordance with natural forces, with no human interference beyond what is required for the preservation of health. The tendency of scientific technique is to cause everything to be regarded as not just a brute datum, but raw material for the carrying out of some human purpose. The child, and even the embryo, will come to be viewed more and more in this way as the mentality connected with scientific technique becomes more dominant. In this, as in all other forms of scientific power, there are possibilities of good and possibilities of evil. Science alone will not decide which is to prevail.

CHAPTER X

Technique in Psychology

AT the period when I received what was in those days called an education, psychology was still, to all intents and purposes, a branch of philosophy. Mental events were divided into knowing, willing, and feeling. Attempts were made to define perception and sensation, and in general the subject was one for verbal analysis of concepts that the philosophers had rendered familiar though not intelligible. It is true that every text-book began with an account of the brain, but having given that account, it made no further allusion to it. It is true also that there existed a form of psychology which made use of laboratories and attempted to be very scientific. This form was practised especially by Wundt and his disciples. You showed a man a picture of a dog, and said: "What's that?" You then measured carefully how long it took him to say "dog"; in this way much valuable information was amassed. But strange to say, in spite of the apparatus of measurement, it turned out that there was nothing to do with this valuable information except to forget it. Every new science is hampered by too slavish an imitation of the technique of some older science. No doubt measurement is the hall-mark of an exact science, and therefore scientifically-minded psychologists looked about for something measurable connected with their subject-matter. They were wrong, however, in thinking that time intervals were the appropriate thing to measure: this position, as it turned out, is occupied by the saliva of dogs.

Psychology as pursued everywhere in the past (and still at Oxford) was incapable of giving practical control over mental processes, and never aimed at this result. To this general statement there is, however, one important exception, namely psychology as studied by the Society of Jesus. Much that the rest of the world has only recently understood was apprehended by Ignatius Loyola, and impressed by him upon the Order which he founded. The two tendencies which divide progressive psychologists in our day, namely, psycho-analysis and behaviourism, are both equally exemplified in Jesuit practice. I think one may say on the whole that the Jesuits relied mainly on behaviourism for their own training, and upon psycho-analysis for their power over penitents. This, however, is only a matter of degree; the instructions which Loyola gave as regards meditations upon the Passion belong rather with the Freudian than with the Watsonian psychology.

All modern scientific thinking, as we have already had occasion to remark, is at bottom power thinking, that is to say, the fundamental human impulse to which it appeals is the love of power, or, to express the matter in other terms, the desire to be the cause of as many and as large effects as possible. Jesuit thinking was, of course, power thinking in a very crude and direct sense, whereas in true scientific thought the power impulse is refined and sublimated. When the Jesuits knew the technique for a given effect, they were no longer concerned with the mechanism by which that effect came about; so long as the right habits were formed, it was a matter of indifference to them whether they were habits in the larynx or in the adrenal glands. In this respect, remarkable as was their practical understanding, they cannot be regarded as truly scientific psychologists. They practised an art analogous to that of the horse-breaker or the lion-tamer, and so long as their art was successful, they were content. The modern psychologists, on the contrary, like Hamlet, "must be edified by the margent." For this reason hypnotism, important and singular as it is, was long ignored by psychologists because they did not know how to fit it into their scheme. For a long time psychologists did not seem to think that they were called upon to deal with those mental phenomena which could not be regarded as rational, such as dreams, hysteria, insanity, and hypnotism. Man was a rational animal, and the purpose of psychology was to make us think well of him. Strange to say, so long as this view persisted, psychology made no progress. Educational progress came from attempts to teach the feeble-minded, and psychological progress from attempts to understand lunatics. The feeble-minded, it was admitted, were not necessarily wicked when they failed to learn, and were not therefore to be stimulated into intelligence by flogging. From experience of the feeble-minded certain persons of transcendent genius arrived at the inference that perhaps the normal intelligence also is not best stimulated by flogging. A similar transformation was brought about in the psychology of belief by the study of the insane. The opinions of the insane, it was found, are not arrived at by a series of syllogisms, having major premises which are universally admitted; but in the eighteenth century it was supposed that men of normal intelligence did arrive at their opinions in this way. I do not mean to say that men of normal intelligence supposed this about each other; I mean only that the theoretical psychologists supposed it. When Voltaire's Cacambo is confronted by a horde of cannibals, who proceed to make preparations for eating him, he makes them a set speech beginning "Gentlemen," in which he deduces syllogistically from the principles of natural law that they ought only to eat Jesuits, and that since he and Candide are not Jesuits, it would be wrong to roast them. The cannibals find his speech very reasonable, and liberate him and Candide with acclamation. Voltaire here is, of course, making fun of the intellectualism of his age, but his age deserved it, so far at least as the theoretical psychologists were concerned. Nowadays, though this is a quite recent development, theoretical psychologists know as much about mental processes as is known by Jesuits and men of the world. It has been found that the causes of belief in waking life are in the main analogous to those in dreams, or during insanity, or under hypnotism. They are not, of course, wholly analogous: there is a little leaven of reason which makes all the difference, but reason is a cause of disbelief rather than of belief. "Animal faith" supplies what is positive, and reason only what is negative. Science, speaking broadly, is a tree growing from the soil of animal faith, but clipped by the shears of reason; it is the part played by animal faith that modern psychology has begun to understand.

There are in psychology two modern techniques which are as yet more or less antagonistic to each other. There is the technique of Freud, and the technique of Pavlov.

Freud's purposes were primarily therapeutic. He was concerned to cure people of the less extreme forms of mental disorder. In the course of this attempt he was led to a view as to the causation of such troubles. Freud's theory on this subject has proved even more important than his contribution to therapeutics. I think a free rendering of the general principles emerging from the work of Freud and his followers would be more or less as follows. There are in human beings certain fundamental desires, usually in a greater or less degree unconscious, and our mental life is moulded so as to yield the greatest possible satisfaction of these desires. But wherever obstacles arise to their realization, the means adopted for overcoming these obstacles are apt to be somewhat foolish, in the sense that they operate only in the realm of phantasy and not in that of reality. I do not think that psycho-analysts have reflected very deeply upon the distinction between phantasy and reality. I suppose that for practical purposes "phantasy" is what the patient believes, and "reality" is what the analyst believes. Men are not allowed to become recognized analysts until they have become analysed, and in this process it is expected that they will adopt the official view as to reality. If they can convey this in turn to their patients, their view of reality will in the end carry the day, or so at least it may be hoped. Without going into metaphysical subtleties, one may say that reality is that which is generally accepted, while phantasy is that which is believed only by an individual or a group of individuals. This definition cannot, of course, be taken strictly, since, if it were, the opinion of Copernicus, for example, would have been phantasy in his day and reality in the time of Newton. There are, however, a number of opinions which are quite obviously based upon the individual desires of those who hold them, and not upon grounds which make a universal appeal. I was once visited by a man who expressed a desire to study my philosophy, but confessed that in the only book of mine which he had read there was only one statement that he could understand, and that was a statement with which he could not agree. I inquired what the statement was, and he replied: "It is the statement that Julius Cæsar is dead." I naturally asked why he did not accept this statement. He drew himself up and replied rather stiffly: "Because I am Julius Cæsar." Being alone with him in a flat, I took steps to reach the street as soon as possible, since it appeared to me probable that his opinion was not derived from an objective study of reality. This incident illustrates the difference between sane and insane beliefs. Sane beliefs are those inspired by desires which agree with the desires of other men; insane beliefs are those inspired by desires which conflict with those of other men. We should all like to be Julius Cæsar, but we recognize that if one is Julius Cæsar, another is not; therefore the man who thinks he is Julius Cæsar annoys us, and we regard him as mad. We should all like to be immortal, but one man's immortality does not conflict with another's, therefore the man who thinks he is immortal is not mad. Delusions are those opinions which fail to make the necessary social adjustments, and the purpose of psycho-analysis is to produce the social adjustments which will cause such opinions to be abandoned.

The reader, I hope, will have felt that the above account is in some respects inadequate. However hard we may try, it is scarcely possible to escape from the metaphysical conception of "fact." Freud himself, for example, when he first propounded his theory of the pervasiveness of sex, was viewed with the kind of horror that is inspired by a dangerous lunatic. If social adjustment is the test of sanity, he was insane, though when his theories came to be sufficiently accepted to be a source of income, he became sane. This is obviously absurd. Those who agree with Freud must contend that there is objective truth in his theories, not merely that they are such as many people can be got to accept. What remains of the theory of social adjustment as the test of truth is that beliefs inspired by purely personal desires are seldom true; I mean by purely personal desires those that conflict with the interests of others. Take as an illustration the man who becomes rich on the Stock Exchange; his *activities* are, it is true, inspired by the desire to become rich, which is purely personal, but his *beliefs* must be inspired by an impartial survey of the markets. If his *beliefs* are personal, he will lose money, and his desires will not be gratified. As this illustration shows, even our most personal desires are more likely to be gratified if our beliefs are impersonal than if they are personal. This is the reason why science and scientific method are held in esteem. When I say that a belief is impersonal I mean that those desires which enter into its causation are universal human desires, and not such as are peculiar to the person in question.

Psycho-analysis as a psychological theory consists in the discovery of the desires, usually unconscious, which inspire belief, especially in dreams and in insane delusions, but also in all the less rational parts of our nominally sane working life. Considered as a therapeutic, psycho-analysis is a technique which aims at substituting impersonal for personal desires as sources of belief wherever personal desires have become so dominant as to interfere with social behaviour. The technique of psycho-analysis where adults are concerned is as yet slow, cumbrous, and expensive. The most important applications of psycho-analytic theory are to education. These applications are as yet in an experimental stage, and owing to the hostility of the authorities they can only be made on a very small scale.[1] It is, however, already evident that moral and emotional education has hitherto been conducted on wrong lines, and has produced maladjustments which have been sources of cruelty, timidity, stupidity, and other unfortunate mental characteristics. I think it possible that psycho-analytic theory may be absorbed into something more scientific, but I do not doubt that something of what psycho-analysis has to suggest in regard to education will be found permanently valid and of immense importance.

The behaviourist psychology, which has its experimental basis mainly in the work of Pavlov, but has become generally known through Dr. John B. Watson, is at first sight very different from psycho-analysis and scarcely compatible with it. I am persuaded, however, that there is truth in both, and that it is important to arrive at a synthesis of the two. Freud starts from fundamental desires, such as the sexual impulse, which he conceives as seeking an outlet now in one direction, now in another. Behaviourism starts with an apparatus of reflexes and the process of conditioning. There is perhaps not quite so much difference as there seems to be. The reflex corresponds roughly to Freud's fundamental desires, and the process of conditioning to the search for different outlets. As a technique for acquiring power, behaviourism is, I think, superior to psycho-analysis: it embodies the methods

---

[1] For experimental data on this subject see Susan Isaacs, *The Intellectual Growth in Young Children*, 1930.

which have always been adopted by those who train animals or drill soldiers; it utilizes the force of habit, the strength of which has always been recognized; and, as we saw when we were considering Pavlov, it makes it possible both to cause and to cure neurasthenia and hysteria. The conflicts which appear in psycho-analysis as emotional re-appear in behaviourism as conflicts between habits, or between a habit and a reflex. If a child were severely beaten every time it sneezed, it is probable that a phantasy world would in time build itself up in his mind around the conception of sneezing; he would dream of Heaven as a place where the spirits of the blest sneeze unceasingly, or on the contrary he might think of Hell as a place of punishment for those who live in open sternutation. In this sort of way the problems brought to the fore by psycho-analysis can, I think, be dealt with on behaviourist lines. At the same time it should be admitted that these problems, whose importance is very great, would probably not have come to the fore but for the psycho-analytic approach. For the practical purposes of educational technique, I think it will be found that the educator should behave as a psycho-analyst when he is concerned with matters touching powerful instincts, but as a behaviourist in matters which a child views as emotionally unimportant. For example, affection for parents should be viewed in the psycho-analytic manner, but brushing teeth in the behaviourist manner.

So far we have been considering those ways of influencing the mental life which proceed by mental means

as in psycho-analysis, or by means of the conditioned reflex as in behaviourism. There are, however, other methods
which may in time prove of immense importance. These
are the methods which operate through physiological
means, such as the administering of drugs. The curing
of cretinism by means of iodine is so far the most remarkable of these methods. In Switzerland all salt for human
consumption is obliged by law to be iodized, and this
measure has been found adequate as a preventive of
cretinism. The work of Cannon and others concerning
the influence of the ductless glands upon the emotions
has become widely known, and it is clear that by administering artificially the substances which the ductless glands
provide, a profound effect can be produced upon temperament and character. The effects of alcohol, opium,
and various other drugs have long been familiar, but these
effects are on the balance harmful unless the drug is taken
with unusual moderation. There is, however, no *a priori*
reason why drugs should not be discovered which have a
wholly beneficial effect. I have never myself observed
any but good effects to flow from the drinking of tea, at
any rate if it is China tea. It is possible also that psychological marvels may become possible through pre-natal
treatment. One of the most eminent philosophers of our
day regards his superiority to his brothers, perhaps hu-
morously, as due to the fact that shortly before his birth
his mother was in a carriage which rolled down the
Simplon in an accident. I do not suggest that this method
should be adopted in the hope of turning us all into

philosophers, but perhaps in time we shall discover some more peaceable means of endowing the fœtus with intelligence. Education used to begin at eight years old with the learning of the Latin declensions; now, under the influence of psycho-analysis, it begins at birth. It is to be expected that with the advance of experimental embryology the important part of education will be found to be prenatal. This is already the case with fishes and newts, but in regard to them the scientist is not hampered by education authorities.

The power of psychological technique to mould the mentality of the individual is still in its infancy, and is not yet fully realized. There can, I think, be little doubt that it will increase enormously in the near future. Science has given us, in succession, power over inanimate nature, power over plants and animals, and finally power over human beings. Each power involves its own kind of dangers, and perhaps the dangers involved in power over human beings are the greatest, but that is a matter that we will consider at a later stage.

CHAPTER XI

Technique in Society

THE application of science to social questions is even more recent than its application to individual psychology. There are, it is true, a few directions in which a scientific attitude is to be found as early as the beginning of the nineteenth century. Malthus's theory of population, whether true or false, is certainly scientific. The arguments by which he supports it are not appeals to prejudice, but to population statistics and the expenses of agriculture. Adam Smith and Ricardo are also scientific in their economics. Again, I do not mean to say that the theories they advance are invariably true, but that their outlook and their type of reasoning has the characteristics which distinguish scientific method. From Malthus came Darwin, and from Darwin came Darwinism, which as applied to politics has turned out to be far from scientific. The phrase "survival of the fittest" proved too much for the intellects of those who speculate on social questions. The word "fittest" seems to have ethical implications, from which it follows that the nation, race, and class to which a writer belongs must necessarily be the fittest. Hence we arrive, under the ægis of a pseudo-Darwinian philosophy, at doctrines such as the Yellow Peril, Australia for the Australians, and the superiority of the Nordic race. On account of the ethical bias, one must view all Darwinian arguments on social questions with the greatest suspicion. This applies not only as between different races, but also as between different classes in the same nation. All Darwinian writers belong to the professional classes, and it is therefore an accepted maxim of Darwinian politics that the professional classes are biologically the most desirable. It follows that their sons ought to get a better education at the public expense than that which is given to the sons of wage-earners. In all such arguments it is impossible to see an application of science to practical affairs. There is merely a borrowing of some of the language of science for the purpose of making prejudice seem respectable.

There is, however, a large amount of genuine experimental science in social affairs. Perhaps the most important set of experiments in this realm is that which we owe to advertisers. This material, valuable as it is, has not been utilized by experimental psychologists, because it belongs to a region remote from the Universities, and they would feel themselves vulgarized by contact with anything so gross. But anybody who is in earnest in studying the psychology of belief cannot do better than consult the great advertising firms. No test of belief is so searching as the financial one. When a man is willing to back his belief by spending money in accordance with it, his belief must be regarded as genuine. Now this is precisely the test which the advertiser is perpetually applying. Various people's soaps are recommended in various ways; some of these ways produce the desired result, others do not, or at any rate not to the same degree. Clearly the advertisement which causes a man's soap to be bought is more effective in creating belief than the one which does not. I do not think any experienced advertiser would suggest that the merits of the respective soaps had any share whatever in bringing about the result. Very large sums of money are paid to the men who invent good advertisements, and rightly so, for the power to cause large numbers of people to believe what you assert is a very valuable power. Consider its importance, for example, to the founders of religions. In the past they often had to adopt the most painful forms of publicity. How much pleasanter their lives would have been if they could have gone to an agent who would have purchased the respect of their disciples in return for a percentage on the ecclesiastical revenues!

From the technique of advertising it seems to follow that in the great majority of mankind any proposition will win acceptance if it is reiterated in such a way as to remain in the memory. Most of the things that we believe we believe because we have heard them affirmed; we do not remember where or why they were affirmed, and we are therefore unable to be critical even when the affirmation was made by a man whose income would be increased by its acceptance and was not backed by any evidence whatever. Advertisements tend, therefore, as the technique becomes perfected, to be less and less argumentative, and more and more merely striking. So long as an impression is made, the desired result is achieved.

Considered scientifically, advertisements have another great merit, which is that their effects, so far as is known through the receipts of the advertisers, are mass effects, not effects upon individuals, so that the data acquired are data as to mass psychology. For the purposes of studying society rather than individuals, advertisements are therefore invaluable. Unfortunately their purpose is practical rather than scientific. For scientific purposes I suggest the following experiment. Let two soaps, A and B, be manufactured, of which A is excellent and B abominable; let A be advertised by stating its chemical composition and by testimonials from eminent chemists; let B be advertised by the bare statement that it is the best, accompanied by the portraits of famous Hollywood beauties. If man is a rational animal, more of A will be sold than of B. Does anyone, in fact, believe that this would be the result?

The advantages of advertisement have come to be realized pretty fully by politicians, but are only beginning to be realized by the Churches; when the Churches become more fully alive to its advantages as compared with the traditional religious technique (which dates from before the invention of printing), we may hope for a great revival of faith. On the whole, the Soviet Government and the Communist religion are those which hitherto have best understood the use of advertisement. They are, it is true, somewhat hampered by the fact that most Russians cannot read; this obstacle, however, they are doing their best to remove.

This consideration brings us naturally to the subject of education, which is the second great method of public propaganda. Education has two very different purposes: on the one hand it aims at developing the individual and giving him knowledge which will be useful to him; on the other hand it aims at producing citizens who will be convenient for the State or the Church which is educating them. Up to a point these two purposes coincide in practice: it is convenient to the State that citizens should be able to read, and that they should possess some technical skill in virtue of which they are able to do productive work; it is convenient that they should possess sufficient moral character to abstain from unsuccessful crime, and sufficient intelligence to be able to direct their own lives. But when we pass beyond these elementary requirements, the interests of the individual may often conflict with those of the State or the Church. This is especially the case in regard to credulity. To those who control publicity, credulity is an advantage, while to the individual a power of critical judgment is likely to be beneficial; consequently the State does not aim at producing a scientific habit of mind, except in a small minority of experts, who are well paid, and therefore, as a rule, supporters of the *status quo*. Among those who are not well paid credulity is more advantageous to the State; consequently children in school are taught to believe what they are told and are punished if they express disbelief. In this way a conditioned reflex is established, leading to a belief in anything said authoritatively by elderly persons of importance. You and I, reader, owe our immunity from spoliation to this beneficent precaution on the part of our respective Governments.

One of the purposes of the State in education is certainly, on the whole, beneficent. The purpose in question is that of producing social coherence. In mediæval Europe, as in modern China, the lack of social coherence proved disastrous. It is difficult for large masses of men to co-operate as much as is necessary for their own welfare. The tendency to anarchy and civil war is always one to be guarded against, except on those rare occasions when some great principle is at stake which is of sufficient importance to make civil war worth while. For this reason that part of education which aims at producing loyalty to the State is to be praised in so far as it is directed against internal anarchy. But in so far as it is directed to the perpetuation of international anarchy, it is bad. On the whole, at present in education, the form of loyalty to the State which is most emphasized is hostility to its enemies. No one was shocked when in the first half of 1914 the Northern Irish wished to fight against the British Government, but everyone was shocked when in the second half of the same year some of the Southern Irish wished not to fight against the Germans.

Modern inventions and modern technique have had a powerful influence in promoting uniformity of opinion and making men less individual than they used to be. Read, for example, *The Stammering Century* by Gilbert Seldes, and compare it with America at the present day. In the nineteenth century new sects were perpetually springing up, new prophets were founding communities in the wilderness; celibacy, polygamy, free love, all had their devotees, consisting not of single cranks, but of whole cities. A somewhat similar mental condition existed in Germany in the sixteenth century, in England in the seventeenth, and in Russia until the establishment of the Soviet Government. But in the modern world there are three great sources of uniformity in addition to education: these are the Press, the cinema, and the radio.

The Press has become an agent of uniformity as a result of technical and financial causes: the larger the circulation of a newspaper, the higher the rate it can charge for its advertisements and the lower the cost of printing per copy. A foreign correspondent costs just as much whether his newspaper has a large or a small circulation; therefore his relative cost is diminished by every increase in circulation. A newspaper with a large circulation can hire the most expensive legal talent to defend it against libel suits, and can often conceal from all but serious students its misstatements of facts. For all these reasons, of which advertisements are the chief, big newspapers tend to defeat small ones. There are, of course, small weeklies to please small sets of cranks or high-brows, and there are journals devoted to special interests, such as yachting or fly-fishing, but the immense majority of newspaper readers confine themselves either, as in England, to a small number of newspapers, or, as in America, to a small number of syndicated groups of newspapers. The difference between England and America in this respect is, of course, due to size. In England, if Lord Rothermere and Lord Beaverbrook desire anything to be known, it will be known; if they desire it to be unknown, it will be unknown except to a few pertinacious busybodies. Although there are rival groups in the newspaper world, there are, of course, many matters as to which the rival groups are agreed. In a suburban train in the morning, one man may be reading the *Daily Mail* and another the *Daily Express*, but if by some miracle they should fall into conversation they would not find much divergence in the opinions they had imbibed or in the facts of which they had been informed. Thus for reasons which are ultimately technical and scientific, the newspapers have become an influence tending to uniformity and increasing the rarity of unusual opinions.

Another modern invention tending towards uniformity is the radio. This, of course, is more the case in England, where it is a Government monopoly, than in America, where it is free. During the General Strike in 1926 it afforded practically the only method of disseminating news. This method was utilized by the Government to state its own case and conceal that of the strikers. I was myself at the time in a remote village, almost the furthest from London, I believe, of any village in England. All the villagers, including myself, assembled in the Post Office every evening to hear the news. A pompous voice would announce: "It is the Home Secretary who has come to make a statement." I regret to say that the villagers all laughed, but if they had been less remote they would probably have been more respectful. In America, where the Government has not interfered with broadcasting, one must expect, if the same policy continues, that there will be a gradual growth of big interests analogous to the big newspapers, and that these will cover as large a proportion of the ground as does the syndicated Press.

But perhaps the most important of all the modern agents of propaganda is the cinema. Where the cinema is concerned, the technical reasons for large-scale organizations leading to almost world-wide uniformity are overwhelming. The costs of a good production are colossal, but are no less if it is exhibited seldom than if it is exhibited often and everywhere. The Germans and the Russians have their own productions, and those of the Russians are, of course, an important part of the Soviet Government's propaganda. In the rest of the civilized world the products of Hollywood preponderate. The great majority of young people in almost all civilized countries derive their ideas of love, of honour, of the way to make money, and of the importance of good clothes, from the evenings spent in seeing what Hollywood thinks good for them. I doubt whether all the schools and churches combined have as much influence as the cinema upon the opinions of the young in regard to such intimate matters as love and marriage and money-making. The producers of Hollywood are the high-priests of a new religion. Let us be thankful for the lofty purity of their sentiments. We learn from them that sin is always punished, and virtue is always rewarded. True, the reward is rather gross, and such as a more old-fashioned virtue might not wholly appreciate. But what of that? We know from the cinema that wealth comes to the virtuous, and from real life that old So-and-so has wealth. It follows that old So-and-so is virtuous, and that the people who say he exploits his employees are slanderers and trouble-makers. The cinema therefore plays a useful part in safeguarding the rich from the envy of the poor.

It is undoubtedly an important fact in the modern world that almost all the pleasures of the poor can only be provided by men possessed of vast capital or by Governments. The reasons for this, as we have seen, are technical, but the result is that any defects in the *status quo* become known only to those who are willing to spend their leisure time otherwise than in amusement; these are, of course, a small minority, and from a political point of view they are at most times negligible. There is, however, a certain instability about the whole system. In the event of unsuccessful war it might break down, and the population, which had grown accustomed to amusements, might be driven by boredom into serious thought. The Russians, when deprived of vodka by war-time prohibition, made the Russian Revolution. What would Western Europeans do if deprived of their nightly drug from Hollywood? The moral of this for Western European Governments is that they must keep on good terms with America. In the American imperialism of the future it may turn out that the producers of cinemas have been the pioneers.

So far we have been considering the effect of scientific technique upon opinions, which cannot be regarded as a wholly cheerful subject. There are, however, many much better effects. Consider, for example, the matter of public health. In 1870 the death-rate in England and Wales was 22.9, and the infant death-rate was 160; in 1929 these had fallen respectively to 13.4 and 74. This change is attributable almost wholly to scientific technique. Improvements in medicine, in hygiene, in sanitation, in diet, have all played their part in the diminution of suffering and unhappiness represented by these bare statistical facts. In old days it was expected that about half the children in a family would die before they grew up; this involved pain, illness, and sorrow to the mother, often great suffering to the children, and a waste of natural resources in the care of children who never lived to become productive. Until the adoption of steam transport by land and sea perpetual famines were inevitable, causing unspeakable anguish in the course of a slow destruction of human life. And not only did people, even in ordinary times, die at a much greater rate than they do now, but they were far more often ill. Nowadays in the West typhus is unknown, smallpox very rare, tuberculosis usually curable; these three facts alone represent a contribution to human welfare which outweighs any harm that science may have hitherto done in the way of increasing the horrors of war.

Whether the balance in this respect will continue to be on the right side in the future is, of course, an open question, but certainly it has been on the right side hitherto.

It is the fashion among intellectuals to regard our age as one of weariness and discouragement; to them, no doubt, it is so, since they have less influence on affairs than they formerly had, and their whole outlook is more or less inappropriate to modern life. But to the average man, woman, and child this is by no means the case. Great Britain has been passing during the last ten years through an unparalleled economic depression, yet it would seem that the ordinary working-class family has lately been better off than in the prosperous period of forty-five years ago.[1]

The introduction of scientific technique into social affairs is as yet very incomplete and haphazard. Take, for example, the matter of banking and credit. Long ago men took the first step towards scientific technique in this respect when they substituted money for barter; the next step, which did not begin for thousands of years after the introduction of money, was the substitution of banks and credit for cash. Credit has become an immense force controlling the economic life of all advanced communities, but although its principles are fairly well understood by experts, political difficulties stand in the way of the right utilization of these principles, and the barbaric practice of depending upon actual gold is still a cause of much misery. In this, as in other respects, economic forces and technical

[1] In London, weekly earnings in 1928 were 30 per cent. above those of 1886 after taking account of the rise in the cost of living. See *Forty Years of Change*, P. S. King, 1930, p. 130.

requirements demand world-wide organization, but the forces of nationalism present obstacles, and cause people to endure avoidable sufferings patiently because of the pleasure they derive from the thought that foreigners are suffering even more.

The social effect of modern scientific technique is, in practically all directions, to demand an increase both in the size and intensity of organization. When I speak of the intensity of organization I mean the proportion of a man's activities that is governed by the fact of his belonging to some social unit. The primitive peasant may be almost entirely self-directed; he produces his own food, buys very little, and does not send his children to school. The modern man, even if he happens to be an agriculturist, produces only a small proportion of what he eats; if he grows wheat, for example, he probably sells the whole of his crop and buys his bread from the baker like any other man; even if he does not do this, he has to buy most of the rest of his food. In his buying and selling he depends upon immense organizations which are usually international; his reading is provided by the great newspapers, his amusements by Hollywood, the education of his children by the State, his capital, in part at least, by a bank, his political opinions by his Party, his safety and many of his amenities by the Government to which he pays taxes. Thus in all his most important activities he has ceased to be a separate unit and has become dependent upon some social organization. As scientific technique advances, the most profitable size for most organizations increases. In a great many respects national boundaries have become a technical absurdity, and further advance demands that they should be ignored. Unfortunately nationalism is immensely strong, and the increasing power of propaganda which scientific technique has put into the hands of national States is being used to strengthen this anarchic force. Until this state of affairs is amended, scientific technique will not be able to achieve the results of which it is capable in the way of promoting human welfare.

PART THREE

The Scientific Society

CHAPTER XII

Artificially Created Societies

THE scientific society with which the following chapters are to be concerned is, in the main, a thing of the future, although various of its characteristics are adumbrated in various States at the present day. The scientific society, as I conceive it, is one which employs the best scientific technique in production, in education, and in propaganda. But in addition to this, it has a characteristic which distinguishes it from the societies of the past, which have grown up by natural causes, without much conscious planning as regards their collective purpose and structure. No society can be regarded as fully scientific unless it has been created deliberately with a certain structure in order to fulfill certain purposes. This is, of course, a matter of degree. Empires, in so far as they depend upon conquest and are not mere national States, have been created, it may be said, in order to confer glory upon their emperors. But this has been in the past merely a question of the political government, and has made very little difference to the daily life of the people. There are, it is true, semi-mythical lawgivers of the remote past, such as Zoroaster, Lycurgus, and Moses, who are supposed to have impressed their character upon the societies that accepted their authority. In all such cases, however, the laws attributed to them must have been, in the main, pre-existing customs. To take an instance concerning which more is known: the Arabs who accepted the authority of Mahomet made hardly more change in their habits than did Americans when they accepted the Volstead Act. When Mahomet's sceptical relatives decided to throw in their lot with him, they did so because of the smallness of the change that he demanded.

As we approach modern times, the changes deliberately brought about in social structure become greater. This is especially the case where revolutions are concerned. The American Revolution and the French Revolution deliberately created certain societies with certain characteristics, but in the main these characteristics were political, and their effects in other directions formed no part of the primary intentions of the revolutionaries. But scientific technique has so enormously increased the power of governments that it has now become possible to produce much more profound and intimate changes in social structure than any that were contemplated by Jefferson or Robespierre. Science first taught us to create machines; it is now teaching us by Mendelian breeding and experimental embryology to create new plants and animals. There can be little doubt that similar methods will before long give us power, within wide limits, to create new human individuals differing in predetermined ways from the individuals produced by unaided nature. And by means of psychological and economic technique it is becoming possible to create societies as artificial as the steam engine, and as different from anything that would grow up of its own accord without deliberate intention on the part of human agents.

Such artificial societies will, of course, until social science is much more perfected than it is at present, have many unintended characteristics, even if their creators succeed in giving them all the characteristics that were intended. The unintended characteristics may easily prove more important than those that were foreseen, and may cause the artificially constructed societies to break down in one way or another. But I do not think it is open to doubt that the artificial creation of societies will continue and increase so long as scientific technique persists. The pleasure in planned construction is one of the most powerful motives in men who combine intelligence with energy; whatever can be constructed according to a plan, such men will endeavour to construct. So long as the technique for creating a new type of society exists there will be men seeking to employ this technique. They are likely to suppose themselves actuated by some idealistic motive, and it is possible that such motives may play a part in determining what sort of society they shall aim at creating. But the desire to create is not itself idealistic, since it is a form of the love of power, and while the power to create exists there will be men desirous of using this power even if unaided nature would produce a better result than any that can be brought about by deliberate intention.

There are in the world at the present time two Powers which illustrate the possibility of artificial creation. The two Powers in question are Japan and Soviet Russia.

Modern Japan is almost exactly what it was intended to be by the men who made the revolution in 1867. This is one of the most remarkable political achievements in all history, in spite of the fact that the purpose which inspired the innovators was simple and such as every Japanese might be expected to sympathize with. The purpose was, in fact, nothing more recondite than the preservation of national independence. China had been found impotent to resist the Western Powers, and Japan appeared to be in like case. Certain Japanese statesmen perceived that the military and naval power of the Western nations rested upon Western education and Western industrial technique. They decided to introduce both, with such modifications as Japanese history and circumstances demanded. But whereas industrialism had grown up in the West with very little assistance from the State, and scientific knowledge had developed very far before the Western Governments undertook the task of universal education, Japan, being pressed for time, was obliged to impose education and science and industrialism by governmental pressure. It was clearly impossible to effect so great a change in the mentality of the average citizen by mere appeals to reason and self-interest. The reformers, therefore, skilfully enlisted the divine person of the Mikado and the divine authority of the Shinto religion on the side of modern science. The Mikado had been for centuries obscure and unimportant, but he had already been restored to power once before in the year A.D. 645, so that there was a precedent of respectable antiquity for what was being done. The Shinto religion, unlike Buddhism, was indigenous to Japan, but had been for ages thrust into the background by the foreign religion imported from China and Korea. The reformers very wisely decided that in introducing Christian military technique they would not attempt to introduce the theology with which it had hitherto been correlated, but would have a nationalistic theology of their own. Shinto, as now taught by the State in Japan, is a powerful weapon of nationalism; its gods are Japanese, and its cosmogony teaches that Japan was created sooner than other countries. The Mikado is descended from the Sun Goddess, and is therefore superior to the mere earthly rulers of other States. Shinto, as now taught, is so different from the old indigenous beliefs that competent students have described it as a new religion.[1] As a result of this skilful combination of enlightened technique with unenlightened theology, the Japanese have succeeded not merely in repelling the Western menace, but in becoming one of the Great Powers and achieving the third place on the sea.

Japan has shown extraordinary sagacity in the adaptation of science to political needs. Science as an intellectual force is sceptical and somewhat destructive of social coherence, while as a technical force it has precisely the op-

[1] See Professor B. H. Chamberlain, *The Invention of a New Religion*, published by The Rationalist Press Association.

posite qualities. The technical developments due to science have increased the size and intensity of organizations, and have more particularly greatly augmented the power of Governments. Governments have, therefore, good reason to be friendly to science, so long as it can be kept from dangerous and subversive speculations. In the main the men of science have shown themselves amenable. The State favours one set of superstitions in Japan, and another in the West, but the scientists both of Japan and of the West have, with some exceptions, been willing to acquiesce in governmental doctrines, because most of them are citizens first, and servants of truth only in the second place.

In spite of the extraordinary success of Japanese policy, there are certain unintended effects which are likely in time to cause serious difficulties. The sudden change of habits and of conscious opinions has induced a certain nervous strain, at any rate in the urban part of the population. This may produce a tendency to hysteria in time of national stress; indeed, such a tendency was shown in the massacres of Koreans that occurred after the earthquake of Tokio. What is more serious, the position of Japan demands the growth of both industrialism and armaments. Owing to the expense of the latter the industrial workers are poor; they tend, consequently, to acquire a rebellious mentality, and the circumstances of their work make it difficult for them to preserve that close family organization upon which Japanese society is built. If Japan should become engaged in an unsuccessful war, these circumstances might produce a revolution analogous to the Russian Revolution. The present social structure in Japan is likely therefore in time to become unstable, but it may be that the same skill which has rendered possible the triumphant career of Japan throughout the last seventy years will enable the Japanese to adapt themselves to changing circumstances gradually without any violent upheaval. The one thing that seems fairly certain is that, whether gradually or by revolution, the social structure in Japan will have to be profoundly modified. Remarkable as it is, therefore, it is not a perfect example of scientific construction. I do not mean by this that it could have been bettered at the time, but only that it is not in all respects a model for the future.

The attempt at scientific construction which is being made by the Soviet Government is more ambitious than that which was carried through by the Japanese innovators in 1867; it aims at a much greater change in social institutions, and at the creation of a society far more different from anything previously known than is that of Japan. The experiment is still in progress, and only a rash man would venture to predict whether it will succeed or fail; the attitude both of friends and enemies towards it has been singularly unscientific. For my part, I am not anxious to appraise the good or evil in the Soviet system, but merely to point out those elements of deliberate planning which make it so far the most complete example of a scientific society. In the first place, all the major factors of production and distribution are controlled by the State;

in the second place, all education is designed to stimulate activity in support of the official experiment; in the third place, the State does what it can to substitute its religion for the various traditional beliefs which have existed within the territory of the U.S.S.R.; in the fourth place, literature and the Press are controlled by the Government, and are such as are thought likely to help it in its constructive purposes; in the fifth place, the family, in so far as it represents a loyalty which competes with loyalty to the State, is being gradually weakened; in the sixth place, the Five Year Plan is bending the whole constructive energies of the nation to the realization of a certain economic balance and productive efficiency, by means of which it is hoped that a sufficient degree of material comfort will be secured for everyone. In every other society of the world there is enormously less central direction than under the Soviet Government. It is true that during the war the energies of the nations were, to a considerable extent, centrally organized, but everyone knew that this was temporary, and even at its height the organization was not so all-pervasive as it is in Russia. The Five Year Plan, as its name implies, is supposed to be temporary, and to belong to a time of stress not wholly unlike that of the Great War, but it is to be expected that if it succeeds, other plans will take its place, since the central organization of a vast nation's activities is too attractive to the organizers to be abandoned readily.

The Russian experiment may succeed or may fail, but even if it fails, it will be followed by others which will share its most interesting characteristic, namely, the unitary direction of a whole nation's activities. This was impossible in earlier days, since it depends upon the technique of propaganda, i. e., upon universal education, newspapers, the cinema, and the wireless. The State had already been strengthened by railways and the telegraph, which made possible the rapid transmission of news and concentration of troops. In addition to modern methods of propaganda, modern methods of warfare have strengthened the State as against discontented elements; aeroplanes and poison gases have made revolt difficult unless it obtains the support of aeronauts and chemists. Any prudent Government will favour these two classes and take pains to secure their loyalty. As the example of Russia has shown, it is now possible for men of energy and intelligence, if they once become possessed of the governmental machine, to retain power even though at first they may have to face the opposition of the majority of the population. We must therefore increasingly expect to see government falling into the hands of oligarchies, not of birth but of opinion. In countries long accustomed to democracy, the empire of these oligarchies may be concealed behind democratic forms, as was that of Augustus in Rome, but elsewhere their rule will be undisguised. If there is to be scientific experimentation in the construction of new kinds of societies, the rule of an oligarchy of opinion is essential. It may be expected that there will be conflicts between different oligarchies, but that ultimately some one oligarchy will acquire world dominion, and will produce a world-wide organization as complete and elaborate as that now existing in the U.S.S.R.

Such a state of affairs will have both merits and demerits; more important than either, however, is the fact that nothing less will enable a society imbued with scientific technique to survive. Scientific technique demands organization, and the more it becomes perfected, the larger are the organizations that it demands. Quite apart from war, the present depression has made it evident than an international organization of credit and banking is necessary to the prosperity not only of some countries, but of all. The international organization of industrial production is being rendered necessary by the efficiency of modern methods. Modern industrial plants can easily supply, in many directions, much more than the total needs of the world. The result of this, which should be wealth, is in fact poverty, owing to competition. In the absence of competition, the immensely enhanced productivity of labour would enable men to arrive at a just compromise between leisure and goods: they could choose whether they would work six hours a day and be rich, or four hours a day and enjoy only moderate comfort. The advantages of world-wide organization, both in preventing the waste of economic competition and in removing the danger of war, are so great as to be becoming an essential condition for the survival of societies possessing scientific technique. This argument is overwhelming in comparison with all counter-arguments, and renders almost unimportant the question whether life in an organized world State will be more or less satisfactory than life at the present day. For it is only in the direction of an organized world State that the human race can develop unless it abandons scientific technique, and it will not do this except as the result of a cataclysm so severe as to lower the whole level of civilization.

The advantages to be derived from an organized world State are great and obvious. There will be, in the first place, security against war and a saving of almost the whole effort and expense now devoted to competitive armaments: there will be, one must suppose, a single, highly efficient fighting machine, employing mainly aeroplanes and chemical methods of warfare, which will be quite obviously irresistible, and will therefore not be resisted.[1] The central government may be changed from time to time by a palace revolution, but this will only alter the personnel of the figure-heads, not the essential organization of government. The central government will, of course, forbid the propaganda of nationalism, by means of which at present anarchy is maintained, and will put in its place a propaganda of loyalty to the world State. It follows that such an organization, if it can subsist for a generation, will be stable. The gain from an economic point of view will be enormous: there will be no waste in competitive production, no uncertainty as to employment, no poverty, no sudden alternations of good and bad times; every man willing to work will be kept in comfort, and every

[1] Cf. *The Problem of the Twentieth Century: a Study in International Relationships*, by David Davies, 1930.

man unwilling to work will be kept in prison. When owing to any circumstances the work upon which a man has hitherto been employed is no longer required, he will be taught some new kind of work, and will be adequately maintained while he is learning his new trade. Economic motives will be employed to regulate population, which will probably be kept stationary. Almost all that is tragic in human life will be eliminated, and even death will seldom come before old age.

Whether men will be happy in this Paradise I do not know. Perhaps biochemistry will show us how to make any man happy, provided he has the necessaries of life; perhaps dangerous sports will be organized for those whom boredom would otherwise turn into anarchists; perhaps sport will take over the cruelty which will have been banished from politics; perhaps football will be replaced by play battles in the air in which death will be the penalty of defeat. It may be that so long as men are allowed to seek death, they will not mind having to seek it in a trivial cause: to fall through the air before a million spectators may come to be thought a glorious death even if it has no purpose but the amusement of a holiday crowd. It may be that in some such way a safety valve can be provided for the anarchic and violent forces in human nature; or again, it may be that by wise education and suitable diet men may be cured of all their unruly impulses, and all life may become as quiet as a Sunday school.

There will, of course, be a universal language, which will be either Esperanto or pidgin-English. The literature of the past will for the most part not be translated into this language, since its outlook and emotional background will be considered unsettling: serious students of history will be able to obtain a permit from the Government to study such works as *Hamlet* and *Othello*, but the general public will be forbidden access to them on the ground that they glorify private murder; boys will not be allowed to read books about pirates or Red Indians; love themes will be discouraged on the ground that love, being anarchic, is silly, if not wicked. All this will make life very pleasant for the virtuous.

Science increases our power to do both good and harm, and therefore enhances the need for restraining destructive impulses. If a scientific world is to survive, it is therefore necessary that men should become tamer than they have been. The splendid criminal must no longer be an ideal, and submissiveness must be more admired than it has been in the past. In all this there will be both gain and loss, and it is not within human power to strike a balance between the two.

CHAPTER XIII

The Individual and the Whole

THE nineteenth century suffered from a curious division between its political ideas and its economic practice. In politics it carried out the Liberal ideas of Locke and Rousseau, which were adapted to a society of small peasant proprietors. Its watchwords were Liberty and Equality, but meantime it was inventing the technique which is leading the twentieth century to destroy liberty and to replace equality by new forms of oligarchy. The prevalence of Liberal thought has been in some ways a misfortune, since it has prevented men of large vision from thinking out in an impersonal manner the problems raised by industrialism. Socialism and Communism, it is true, are essentially industrial creeds, but their outlook is so much dominated by the class war that they have little leisure to give to anything but the means of achieving political victory. Traditional morality gives very little help in the modern world. A rich man may plunge millions into destitution by some act which not even the severest Catholic confessor would consider sinful, while he will need absolution for a trivial sexual aberration which, at the worst, has wasted an hour that might have been more usefully employed. There is need of a new doctrine on the subject of my duty to my neighbour. It is not only traditional religious teaching that fails to give adequate guidance on this subject, but also the teaching of nineteenth-century Liberalism. Take, for example, such a book as Mill on Liberty. Mill maintains that while the State has a right to interfere with those of my actions that have serious consequences to others, it should leave me free where the effects of my actions are mainly confined to myself. Such a principle, however, in the modern world, leaves hardly any scope for individual freedom. As society becomes more organic, the effects of men upon each other become more and more numerous and important, so that there remains hardly anything in regard to which Mill's defence of liberty is applicable. Take, for example, freedom of speech and of the Press. It is clear that a society that permits these is thereby precluded from various achievements which are possible to a society that forbids them. In time of war this is obvious to everybody, because in war-time the national purpose is simple, and the causation involved is obvious. Hitherto it has not been customary for a nation in peace-time to have any national purpose except the preservation of its territory and its constitution. A government which, like that of Soviet Russia, has a purpose in peace-time as ardent and definite as that of other nations in war-time, is compelled to curtail freedom of speech and of the Press as much while it is at peace as other nations do when they are at war.

The diminution of individual liberty which has been

taking place during the last twenty years is likely to continue, since it has two continuing causes. On the one hand, modern technique makes society more organic; on the other hand, modern sociology makes men more and more aware of the causal laws in virtue of which one man's acts are useful or harmful to another man. If we are to justify any particular form of individual liberty in the scientific society of the future, we shall have to do it on the ground that that form of liberty is for the good of society as a whole, but not in most cases on the ground that the acts concerned affect nobody but the agent.

Let us take some examples of traditional principles which appear no longer defensible. The first example that occurs to me is as regards the investment of capital. At present, within wide limits, any man who has money to invest may invest it as he chooses. This freedom was defended during the heyday of *laissez faire* on the ground that the business which paid best was always the most socially useful. Few men nowadays would dare to maintain such a doctrine. Nevertheless the old freedom persists. It is clear that in a scientific society capital would be invested where its social utility is greatest, not where it earns the highest rate of profits. The rate of profits earned depends often upon quite accidental circumstances. Take, for example, the competition between railways and buses: railways have to pay for their permanent way, while buses do not. It may therefore happen that to the investor railways are unprofitable and buses profitable, even when the exact opposite is the case for the community considered as a whole. Or again, consider the profits of those who had the good sense to acquire property in the neighbourhood of Millbank Prison shortly before it was turned into the Tate Gallery. The expenditure which brought these men their profits was public expenditure, and their profits afford no evidence that they had invested their money in a manner advantageous to the public. To take a more important illustration: consider the immense sums of money that are spent on advertising. It cannot possibly be maintained that these bring any but the most meagre return to the community. The principle of permitting each capitalist to invest his money as he chooses is not, therefore, socially defensible.

Take again such a matter as housing. In England individualism leads most families to prefer a small house of their own rather than an apartment in a large house. The result is that the suburbs of London are spread out through mile after mile of dreariness, to the immense detriment of the women and children. Each housewife cooks an abominable dinner at great expenditure of labour for an infuriated husband. The children, when they come home from school, or while they are too young to go to school, find themselves cooped up in small stuffy premises where either they are a nuisance to their parents or their parents are a nuisance to them. In a more sensible community, each family would occupy a part of an immense building with a courtyard in the middle; there would be no individual cooking, but only communal meals. Children, as soon as they were no longer at the breast, would spend their day in large airy halls under the care of women possessing the knowledge, the training, and the temperament required for making young children happy. The wives, who at present drudge all day doing wasteful work badly, would be set free to earn their living outside the home. The benefit of such a system to the mothers, and still more to the children, would be incalculable. At the Rachel Macmillan nursery school it was found that about 90 per cent. of the children had rickets when they first came, and almost all were cured at the end of the first year in the school. In the ordinary home the necessary modicum of light and air and good food cannot be provided, whereas all these things can be provided quite cheaply if they are provided for many children at once. The freedom to cause one's children to grow up stunted and crippled on the ground that one is too fond of them to part with them is a freedom which is certainly not in the public interest.

Take again the question of work, both the kind of work and the method of performing it. At present young people choose their own trade or profession, usually because at the moment of their choice it seems to afford a good opening. A well-informed person possessed of foresight might know that the particular line in question was going to be much less profitable a few years hence. In such a case some public guidance to the young might prove extremely useful. And as regards technical methods, it is seldom in the public interest that an antiquated or wasteful technique should be allowed to persist when a more economical technique is known. At present, owing to the irrational character of the capitalist system, the interest of the individual wage-earner is very often opposed to the interest of the community, since economical methods may cause him to lose his job. This is due to the survival of capitalistic principles in a society which has grown so organic that it ought not to tolerate them. It is obvious that in a well-organized community it should be impossible for a large body of individuals to profit by preserving an inefficient technique. It is clear that the use of the most efficient technique should be enforced, and no wage-earner should be allowed to suffer by its enforcement.

I come now to a matter which touches the individual more intimately: I mean the question of propagation. It has hitherto been considered that any man and woman not within the prohibited degrees have a right to marry, and having married have a right, if not a duty, to have as many children as nature may decree. This is a right which the scientific society of the future is not likely to tolerate. In any given state of industrial and agricultural technique there is an optimum density of population which ensures a greater degree of material well-being than would result from either an increase or a diminution of numbers. As a general rule, except in new countries, the density of population has been beyond this optimum, though perhaps France, in recent decades, has been an exception. Except where there is property to be inherited, the member of a small family suffers almost as much from over-population as the member of a large family. Those who cause over-population are therefore doing an injury not only to their own children, but to the community. It may therefore be assumed that society will discourage them if necessary, as soon as religious prejudices no longer stand in the way of such action. The same question will arise in a more dangerous form as between different nations and different races. If a nation finds that it is losing military superiority through a lower birth-rate than that of a rival, it may attempt, as has already been done in such cases, to stimulate its own birth-rate; but when this proves ineffective, as it probably will, there will be a tendency to demand a limitation in the birth-rate of the rival nation. An international government, if it ever comes into being, will have to take account of such matters, and just as there is at present a quota of national immigrants into the United States, so in future there will be a quota of national immigrants into the world. Children in excess of the licensed figure will presumably be subjected to infanticide. This would be less cruel than the present method, which is to kill them by war or starvation. I am, however, only prophesying a certain future, not advocating it.

Quality as well as quantity of population is likely to become a matter for public regulation. Already in many States of America it is permissible to sterilize the mentally defective, and a similar proposal in England is in the domain of practical politics. This is only the first step. As time goes on we may expect a greater and greater percentage of the population to be regarded as mentally defective from the point of view of parenthood. However that may be, it is clear that the parents who have a child when there is every likelihood of its being mentally defective are doing a wrong both to the child and to the community. No defensible principle of liberty therefore stands in the way of preventing them from such behaviour.

In suggesting any curtailment of liberty there are always two quite distinct questions to be considered. The first is whether such a curtailment would be in the public interest if it were wisely carried out, and the second is whether it will be in the public interest when it is carried out with a certain measure of ignorance and perversity. These two questions are in theory quite distinct, but from the point of view of the government the second question does not exist, since every government believes itself entirely free from both ignorance and perversity. Every government, consequently, in so far as it is not restrained by traditional prejudices, will advocate more interference with liberty than is wise. When, therefore, as in this chapter, we are considering what interferences with liberty might be theoretically justified, we must hesitate to draw the conclusion that they should be advocated in practice. I think it probable, however, that almost all interferences with liberty for which there is a theoretical justification will, in time, be carried out in practice, because scientific technique is gradually making governments so strong that they need not consider outside opinion. The result of this will be that governments will be able to interfere with individual liberty wherever in their opinion there is a sound reason for so doing, and for the reason just given, this will be much more often than it should be. For this reason scientific technique is likely to lead to a governmental tyranny which may in time prove disastrous.

Equality, like liberty, is difficult to reconcile with scientific technique, since this involves a great apparatus of experts and officials inspiring and controlling vast organizations. Democratic forms may be preserved in politics, but they will not have as much reality as in a community of small peasant proprietors. Officials unavoidably have power. And where many vital questions are so technical that the ordinary man cannot hope to understand them, experts must inevitably acquire a considerable measure of control. Take the question of currency and credit as an example. William Jennings Bryan, it is true, made currency an electoral issue in 1896, but the men who voted for him were men who would have voted for him whatever issue he had selected. At the present time, according to many experts who command respect, incalculable misery is being caused by a wrong handling of the question of currency and credit, but it is impossible to submit this question to the electorate except in some passionate and unscientific form; the only way in which anything can be done is to convince the officials who control the great central banks. So long as these men act honestly and in accordance with tradition, the community cannot control them, since if they are mistaken very few people will know it. To take a less important illustration: everyone who has ever compared British and American methods of handling goods traffic on railways knows that the

American methods are infinitely superior. There are no private trucks, and the trucks of the railways are of standard size capable of carrying forty tons. In England everything is higgledy-piggledy and unsystematic, and the use of private trucks causes great waste. If this were put right, freights could be reduced and consumers would benefit, but this is not a matter upon which elections can be fought, since there would be no obvious gain either to railway companies or to railway workers. If a more uniform system is ever imposed, it will be done not as a result of a democratic demand, but by government officials.

The scientific society will be just as oligarchic under socialism or communism as under capitalism, for even where the forms of democracy exist they cannot supply the ordinary voter with the requisite knowledge, nor enable him to be on the spot at the crucial moment. The men who understand the complicated mechanism of a modern community and who have the habit of initiative and decision must inevitably control the course of events to a very great extent. Perhaps this is even more true in a socialistic State than in any other, for in a socialistic State economic and political power are concentrated in the same hands, and the national organization of the economic life is more complete than in a State where private enterprise exists. Moreover, a socialistic State is likely to have more perfect control than any other over the organs of publicity and propaganda, so that it will have more power of causing men to know what it wishes known, and not to know what it wishes unknown. Equality, therefore, like liberty, is, I fear, no more than a nineteenth-century dream. The world of the future will contain a governing class, probably not hereditary, but more analogous to the government of the Catholic Church. And this governing class, as they acquire increasing knowledge and confidence, will interfere more and more with the life of the individual, and will learn more and more the technique of causing this interference to be tolerated. It may be assumed that their purposes will be excellent, and their conduct honourable; it may be assumed that they will be well informed and industrious; but it cannot, I think, be assumed that they will abstain from the exercise of power merely on the ground that individual initiative is a good thing, or on the ground that an oligarchy is unlikely to consider the true interests of its slaves, for men capable of such self-restraint will not rise to positions of power which, except when they are hereditary, are attained only by those who are energetic and untroubled by doubt. What sort of a world will such a governing class produce? In the following chapters I shall hazard a guess at some part of the answer.

CHAPTER XIV

Scientific Government

WHEN I speak of scientific government I ought, perhaps, to explain what I mean by the term. I do not mean simply a government composed of men of science. There were many men of science in the government of Napoleon, including Laplace, who, however, proved so incompetent that he had to be dismissed in a very short time. I should not consider Napoleon's government scientific while it contained Laplace, or unscientific when it lost him. I should define a government as in a greater or less degree scientific in proportion as it can produce intended results: the greater the number of results that it can both intend and produce, the more scientific it is. The framers of the American Constitution, for example, were scientific in safeguarding private property, but unscientific in attempting to introduce a system of indirect election for the Presidency. The governments which made the Great War were unscientific, since they all fell during the course of it. There was, however, one exception, namely Serbia, which was completely scientific, as the result of the War was exactly what was intended by the Serbian Government which was in power at the time of the Serajevo murders.

Owing to the increase of knowledge, it is possible for governments nowadays to achieve many more intended results than were possible in former times, and it is likely that before very long results which even now are impossible will become possible. The total abolition of poverty, for example, is at the present moment technically possible; that is to say, known methods of production, if wisely organized, would suffice to produce enough goods to keep the whole population of the globe in tolerable comfort. But although this is technically possible, it is not yet psychologically possible. International competition, class antagonisms, and the anarchic system of private enterprise stand in the way, and to remove these obstacles is no light task. The diminution of disease is a purpose which in Western nations encounters fewer obstacles and has therefore been more successfully pursued, but to this purpose also there are great obstacles throughout Asia. Eugenics, except in the form of sterilization of the feebleminded, is not yet practical politics, but may become so within the next fifty years. As we have already seen, it may be superseded, when embryology is more advanced, by direct methods of operating upon the fœtus.

All these are things which, as soon as they become clearly feasible, will make a great appeal to energetic and practical idealists. Most idealists are a mixture of two types, which we may call respectively the dreamer and the manipulator. The pure dreamer is a lunatic, the pure manipulator is a man who cares only for personal power, but the idealist lives in an intermediate position between these two extremes. Sometimes the dreamer preponderates, sometimes the manipulator. William Morris found pleasure in dreaming of "News from Nowhere"; Lenin found no satisfaction until he could clothe his ideas in a garment of reality. Both types of idealist desire a world different from that in which they find themselves, but the manipulator feels strong enough to create it, while the dreamer, feeling baffled, takes refuge in phantasy. It is the manipulative type of idealist who will create the scientific society. Of such men, in our own day, Lenin is the archetype. The manipulative idealist differs from the man of merely personal ambition by the fact that he desires not only certain things for himself, but a certain kind of society. Cromwell would not have been content to have been Lord Lieutenant of Ireland in succession to Strafford, or Archbishop of Canterbury in succession to Laud. It was essential to his happiness that England should be a certain sort of country, not merely that he should be prominent in it. It is this element of impersonal desire which distinguishes the idealist from other men. For men of this type there has been in Russia since the Revolution more scope than in any other country at any other time, and the more scientific technique is perfected the more scope there will be for them everywhere. I fully expect, therefore, that men of this sort will have a predominant part to play in moulding the world during the next two hundred years.

The attitude of what may be called practical idealists among men of science at the present day towards problems of government is very clearly set forth in a leading article in *Nature* (September 6, 1930), from which the following are extracts:

Among the changes which the British Association for the Advancement of Science has witnessed since its formation in 1831 is the gradual disappearance of the demarcation between science and industry. As Lord Melchett pointed out in a recent address, the endeavour to distinguish between pure and applied science has now lost any kind of meaning. No clear distinction is possible between science and industry. The results of research work of the most speculative character often lead to outstanding practical results. Such progressive firms as Imperial Chemical Industries, Ltd., now follow in Great Britain the practice long current in Germany by fostering close contact with the scientific research work of the universities. . . .

If, however, it is true that in the last twenty-five years, science has rapidly assumed the responsibility of leadership in industry, a yet wider responsibility is now demanded of it. Under the conditions of modern civilization the community in general, as well as industry, is dependent upon pure and applied science for its continued progress and prosperity. Under the influence of modern scientific discoveries and their applications, not only in industry but also in many other directions, the whole basis of society is rapidly becoming scientific, and to an increasing extent the problems which confront the national administrator, whether judiciary or executive, involve factors which require scientific knowledge for their solution. . . .

In recent years the rapid growth in the rate of all kinds of international communication and transport has forced on industry an outlook and organization that to an astonishing extent are international. These same forces have, however, enlarged the bounds within which mistaken policies can exert their ill-effects. Recent historical research has demonstrated that the difficult racial problems confronting the Union of South Africa to-day are the result of mistaken policies determined by political prejudices three generations ago. In the modern world the dangers arising from mistakes caused by prejudice and neglect of impartial or scientific inquiry are infinitely more serious. In an age when nearly all the problems of administration and development involve scientific factors, civilization cannot afford to leave administrative control in the hands of those who have no first-hand knowledge of science. . . .

Under modern conditions, therefore, more is required of scientific workers than the mere enlargement of the bounds of knowledge. They can no longer be content to allow others to take the results of their discoveries and use them unguided. Scientific workers must accept responsibility for the control of the forces which have been re-

leased by their work. Without their help, efficient administration and a high degree of statesmanship are virtually impossible.

The practical problem of establishing a right relationship between science and politics, between knowledge and power, or more precisely between the scientific worker and the control and administration of the life of the community, is one of the most difficult confronting democracy. The community is, however, entitled to expect from members of the British Association some consideration of such a problem and some guidance as to the means by which science can assume its place of leadership. . . .

It is significant that, in contrast to the relative impotence of scientific workers in national affairs, in the international sphere advisory committees of experts have since the War exerted a remarkable and effective influence even when devoid of all legislative authority. To committees of experts organized by the League of Nations, and exercising advisory functions only, is due the credit of the schemes which were successful in rescuing a European State from bankruptcy and chaos, and in handling an unemployment scheme which settled a million and a half refugees, following upon the greatest migration in history. These examples sufficiently demonstrate that, given the requisite stimulus and enthusiasm, the scientific expert can already exert an effective influence when normal administrative effort has failed, and when indeed, as in the case of Austria, the problem had been dismissed by statesmen as hopeless.

In truth, scientific workers occupy a privileged position in society as well as industry, and there are welcome signs that this is now recognized by scientific workers themselves. Thus, in his presidential address to the Chemical Society (at Leeds) last year, Professor Jocelyn Thorpe suggested that the age is at hand in which the changing majorities of governments will no longer be able to determine major policies, except in directions approved by organized industry, and, in advocating the closer organization of science and industry, stressed the political strength to be obtained thereby. The paper to be read before the British Association on "The Screening of Southend from Gunfire" is further evidence that scientific workers are accepting the responsibility of leadership in matters of social and industrial safety. Whatever inspiration or encouragement the meetings of the British Association may give to scientific workers in the prosecution of their researches, there is no way in which the Association can more fittingly serve humanity than by calling scientific workers to accept those wide responsibilities of leadership in society as well as in industry which their own efforts have made their inevitable lot.

It will be seen from the above that men of science are becoming conscious of the responsibility towards society conferred by their knowledge, and are feeling it a duty to take a larger part in the direction of public affairs than they have hitherto done.

The man who dreams of a scientifically organized

world and wishes to translate his dream into practice finds himself faced with many obstacles. There is the opposition of inertia and habit: people wish to continue behaving as they always have behaved, and living as they always have lived. There is the opposition of vested interest: an economic system inherited from feudal times gives advantages to men who have done nothing to deserve them, and these men, being rich and powerful, are able to place formidable obstacles in the way of fundamental change. In addition to these forces, there are also hostile idealisms. Christian ethics is in certain fundamental respects opposed to the scientific ethic which is gradually growing up. Christianity emphasizes the importance of the individual soul, and is not prepared to sanction the sacrifice of an innocent man for the sake of some ulterior good to the majority. Christianity, in a word, is unpolitical, as is natural since it grew up among men devoid of political power. The new ethic which is gradually growing in connexion with scientific technique will have its eye upon society rather than upon the individual. It will have little use for the superstition of guilt and punishment, but will be prepared to make individuals suffer for the public good without inventing reasons purporting to show that they deserve to suffer. In this sense it will be ruthless, and according to traditional ideas immoral, but the change will have come about naturally through the habit of viewing society as a whole rather than as a collection of individuals. We view a human body as a whole, and if, for example, it is necessary to amputate a limb we do not consider it necessary to prove first that the limb is wicked. We consider the good of the whole body a quite sufficient argument. Similarly the man who thinks of society as a whole will sacrifice a member of society for the good of the whole, without much consideration for that individual's welfare. This has always been the practice in war, because war is a collective enterprise. Soldiers are exposed to the risk of death for the public good, although no one suggests that they deserve death. But men have not hitherto attached the same importance to social purposes other than war, and have therefore shrunk from inflicting sacrifices which were felt to be unjust. I think it probable that the scientific idealists of the future will be free from this scruple, not only in time of war, but in time of peace also. In overcoming the difficulties of the opposition that they will encounter, they will find themselves organized into an oligarchy of opinion such as is formed by the Communist Party in the U.S.S.R.

But, the reader will say, how is all this to come about? Is it not merely a phantasy of wish-fulfilment, utterly remote from practical politics? I do not think so. The future which I foresee is, to begin with, only very partially in agreement with my own wishes. I find pleasure in splendid individuals rather than in powerful organizations, and I fear that the place for splendid individuals will be much more restricted in the future than in the past. Apart from this purely personal opinion, it is easy to imagine ways in which the world might acquire a scientific government such as I am supposing. It is clear that in the next great war Europe will go to pieces. Probably the population will be halved, and the surviving half will be in a condition of anarchic despair. In these circumstances it will rest with the United States to make the world safe for plutocracy. An essential step in this process will be the acquisition of a considerable measure of control over Europe. Dawes Plans and Young Plans, more drastic than those imposed on Germany in recent years, will be imposed upon Europe as a whole; scientific experts will be employed to make Europeans work and to introduce the most up-to-date organization and technique. American marines will occupy the site of what had been London, and skyscrapers will be erected over the ruins of St. Paul's. In this way a world government will come about, in which the power will belong to great plutocrats, but will be largely delegated by them to experts of various types. It may be assumed that the plutocrats, having become soft, will gradually become lazy. Like the Merovingian Kings, they will allow their powers to be usurped by the less lordly experts, and gradually these experts will come to form the real government of the world. I imagine them forming a close corporation, regulated partly by opinion so long as their government is challenged, but chosen later on by means of examinations, intelligence-tests, and tests of will-power.

The society of experts which I am imagining will embrace all eminent men of science except a few wrong-headed and anarchical cranks. It will possess the sole up-to-date armaments, and will be the repository of all new secrets in the art of war. There will, therefore, be no more war, since resistance by the unscientific will be doomed to obvious failure. The society of experts will control propaganda and education. It will teach loyalty to the world government, and make nationalism high treason. The government, being an oligarchy, will instil submissiveness into the great bulk of the population, confining initiative and the habit of command to its own members. It is possible that it may invent ingenious ways of concealing its own power, leaving the forms of democracy intact, and allowing the plutocrats to imagine that they are cleverly controlling these forms. Gradually, however, as the plutocrats become stupid through laziness, they will lose their wealth; it will pass more and more into public ownership and be controlled by the government of experts. Thus, whatever the outward forms may be, all real power will come to be concentrated in the hands of those who understand the art of scientific manipulation.

All this is, of course, a fancy picture, and whatever really happens in the future is likely to be something which cannot be foreseen. It may be that a scientific civilization will be found essentially unstable. There are several reasons which make this a not unplausible view. The most obvious of these is war. It happens that recent innovations in the art of war have increased the power of the attack much more than the power of defence, and there seems no likelihood that the arts of defence will be able to recover lost ground before the next great war. There are those who say that in the next great war nobody will be allowed to be neutral.[1] If that is so, the only hope for the survival of civilization is that some one nation will be sufficiently remote from the theatre of operations and sufficiently strong to emerge with its social structure undestroyed. The United States has the best chance of occupying this position; China also has a certain chance, because of its vast population and of its capacity for enduring anarchy. If these two nations share the universal disintegration which the next war is almost certain to produce in Europe, it is likely to be many centuries before civilization returns to its present level. Even if America survives intact, it will be necessary to set about at once organizing the world government, since civilization could not be expected to survive the shock of yet another world war. In such circumstances, the most important force on the side of civilization will be the desire of American investors to find safe investments in the devastated countries of the old world. Should they be content with investments in their own continent, the outlook would be black indeed.

Another reason for doubting the stability of a scientific civilization is to be derived from the fall of the birth-rate. The most intelligent classes in the most scientific nations are dying out, and the Western nations as a whole do not do much more than reproduce their own numbers. Unless very radical measures are adopted, the white population of the globe will soon begin to diminish. The French have already been led to depend upon African troops, and if the white population dwindles there will be an increasing

[1] See Major Karl Axel Bratt, *That Next War*, 1930.

tendency to leave the rough work to men of other races. In the long run this will lead to mutinies, and reduce Europe to the condition of Haiti. In such circumstances it would be left to China and Japan to carry on our scientific civilization, but in proportion as they acquire it, they, too, will acquire a lowered birth-rate. It is therefore impossible for a scientific civilization to be stable unless artificial methods are adopted for stimulating breeding. There are powerful obstacles in the way of adoption of such methods, both financial and sentimental. In this matter, as in the matter of war, scientific civilization will have to become more scientific if it is to escape destruction. Whether it will become more scientific with sufficient rapidity it is impossible to foresee.

We have seen that scientific civilization demands world-wide organization if it is to be stable. We have considered the possibility of such an organization in matters of government. We shall now consider it in the economic sphere. At present, production is organized as far as possible nationally by means of tariff walls; every nation tries to produce at home as much as possible of the goods that it consumes. This tendency is on the increase, and even Great Britain, which has hitherto aimed at maximizing its exports by means of Free Trade, appears to be on the point of abandoning this policy in favour of comparative economic isolation.

It is, of course, clear that, from a purely economic point of view, it is wasteful to organize production nationally rather than internationally. It would be an economy if all the motor-cars used throughout the world were manufactured in Detroit. That is to say, a car of given excellence could be produced with less expense of human labour in that case than it can at present. In a world scientifically organized, most industrial products would be thus localized. There would be one place for making pins and needles, another place for making scissors and knives, another place for making aeroplanes, and yet another for agricultural machinery. When, if ever, the world government that we have considered comes into being, one of its first tasks will be the international organization of production. Production will no longer be left, as at present, to private enterprise, but will be undertaken solely in accordance with government orders. This is already the case with such things as battleships, because in regard to war efficiency is thought to be important; but in most matters production is left to the chaotic impulses of private manufacturers, who make too much of some things and too little of others, with the result that there is poverty in the midst of unused plenty. The industrial plant at present existing in the world is in many directions far in excess of the world's needs. By eliminating competition and concentrating production in a single concern, all this waste could be avoided.

The control of raw materials is a matter which in any scientific society would be governed by a central authority. At present the important raw materials are controlled by military power. The weak nation possessed of oil soon finds itself under the suzerainty of some stronger nation.

The Transvaal lost its independence because it contained gold. Raw materials ought not to belong to those who, by conquest or diplomacy, have happened to acquire the territory in which they are; they ought to belong to a world authority which would ration them to those who had the most skill in utilizing them. Moreover, our present economic system causes everybody to be wasteful of raw materials, since there is no motive for foresight. In a scientific world the supply of any vital raw material will be carefully estimated, and as the moment of its exhaustion approaches scientific research will be directed to the discovery of a substitute.

Agriculture, for reasons which we considered in an earlier chapter, may have less importance in the future than it has at present, and has had in the past. We shall have not only artificial silk but artificial wool and artificial timber and artificial rubber. In time we may have artificial food. But in the meantime agriculture will become more and more industrialized, both in its methods and in the mentality of those who practise it. American and Canadian agriculturists have already the industrial mentality, not the mentality of the patient peasant. Machinery will, of course, be increasingly employed. In the neighbourhood of large urban markets intensive cultivation with artificial methods of warming the soil will yield many crops every year. Here and there throughout the country-side there will be large power stations forming the nucleus around which the population will cluster. Of agricultural mentality, as it has been known since ancient times, nothing will survive, since the soil and even the climate will be subject to human control.

It may be assumed that every man and woman will be obliged to work, and will be taught a new trade if for any reason work at the old trade is no longer required. The pleasantest work, of course, will be that which gives the most control over the mechanism. The posts giving most power will presumably be awarded to the ablest men as a result of intelligence tests. For entirely inferior work negroes will be employed wherever possible. One may, I suppose, assume that the most desirable kinds of work will be more highly paid than the less desirable kinds, since they require more skill. The society will not be one in which there is equality, although I doubt whether the inequalities will be hereditary except as between different races, i. e., between white and coloured labour. Everybody will be comfortable, and those who occupy the better-paid posts will be able to enjoy considerable luxury. There will not be, as at present, fluctuations of good and bad times, for these are merely the result of our anarchic economic system. Nobody will starve, and nobody will suffer the economic anxieties which at present beset rich and poor alike. On the other hand, life will be destitute of adventure except for the most highly paid experts. Ever since civilization began men have been seeking security more avidly than they have sought anything else. In such a world they will have it, but I am not quite sure whether they will think it worth the price that they will have paid for it.

CHAPTER XV

Education in a Scientific Society

EDUCATION has two purposes: on the one hand to form the mind, on the other hand to train the citizen. The Athenians concentrated on the former, the Spartans on the latter. The Spartans won, but the Athenians were remembered.

Education in a scientific society may, I think, be best conceived after the analogy of the education provided by the Jesuits. The Jesuits provided one sort of education for the boys who were to become ordinary men of the world, and another for those who were to become members of the Society of Jesus. In like manner, the scientific rulers will provide one kind of education for ordinary men and women, and another for those who are to become holders of scientific power. Ordinary men and women will be expected to be docile, industrious, punctual, thoughtless, and contented. Of these qualities probably contentment will be considered the most important. In order to produce it, all the researches of psycho-analysis, behaviourism, and biochemistry will be brought into play. Children will be educated from their earliest years in the manner which is found least likely to produce complexes.

Almost all will be normal, happy, healthy boys or girls. Their diet will not be left to the caprices of parents, but will be such as the best biochemists recommend. They will spend much time in the open air, and will be given no more book-learning than is absolutely necessary. Upon the temperament so formed, docility will be imposed by the methods of the drill-sergeant, or perhaps by the softer methods employed upon Boy Scouts. All the boys and girls will learn from an early age to be what is called "co-operative," i. e., to do exactly what everybody is doing. Initiative will be discouraged in these children, and insubordination, without being punished, will be scientifically trained out of them. Their education throughout will be in great part manual, and when their school years come to an end they will be taught a trade. In deciding what trade they are to adopt, experts will appraise their aptitudes. Formal lessons, in so far as they exist, will be conducted by means of the cinema or the radio, so that one teacher can give simultaneous lessons in all the classes throughout a whole country. The giving of these lessons will, of course, be recognized as a highly skilled undertaking, reserved for the members of the governing class. All that will be required locally to replace the present-day school-teacher will be a lady to keep order, though it is hoped that the children will be so well-behaved that they will seldom require this estimable person's services.

Those children, on the other hand, who are destined to become members of the governing class will have a very different education. They will be selected, some before birth, some during the first three years of life, and a few between the ages of three and six. All the best-known science will be applied to the simultaneous development of intelligence and will-power.

Eugenics, chemical and thermal treatment of the embryo, and diet in early years will be used with a view to the production of the highest possible ultimate ability. The scientific outlook will be instilled from the moment that a child can talk, and throughout the early impressionable years the child will be carefully guarded from contact with the ignorant and unscientific. From infancy up to twenty-one, scientific knowledge will be poured into him, and at any rate from the age of twelve upwards he will specialize in those sciences for which he shows the most aptitude. At the same time he will be taught physical toughness; he will be encouraged to roll naked in the snow, to fast occasionally for twenty-four hours, to run many miles on hot days, to be bold in all physical adventures and uncomplaining when he suffers physical pain. From the age of twelve upwards he will be taught to organize children slightly younger than himself, and will suffer severe censure if groups of such children fail to follow his lead. A sense of his high destiny will be constantly set before him, and loyalty towards his order will be so axiomatic that it will never occur to him to question it. Every youth will thus be subjected to a threefold training: in intelligence, in self-command, and in command over others. If he should fail in any one of these three, he will suffer the terrible penalty of degradation to the ranks of common workers, and will be condemned for the rest of his life to associate with men and women vastly inferior to himself in education and probably in intelligence. The spur of this fear will suffice to produce industry in all but a very small minority of boys and girls of the governing class.

Except for the one matter of loyalty to the world State and to their own order, members of the governing class will be encouraged to be adventurous and full of initiative. It will be recognized that it is their business to improve scientific technique, and to keep the manual workers contented by means of continual new amusements. As those upon whom all progress depends, they must not be unduly tame, nor so drilled as to be incapable of new ideas. Unlike the children destined to be manual workers, they will have personal contact with their teacher, and will be encouraged to argue with him. It will be his business to prove himself in the right if he can, and, if not, to acknowledge his error gracefully. There will, however, be limits to intellectual freedom, even among the children of the governing class. They will not be allowed to question the value of science, or the division of the population into manual workers and experts. They will not be allowed to coquette with the idea that perhaps poetry is as valuable as machinery, or love as good a thing as scientific research. If such ideas do occur to any venturesome spirit, they will be received in a pained silence, and there will be a pretence that they have not been heard.

A profound sense of public duty will be instilled into

boys and girls of the governing class as soon as they are able to understand such an idea. They will be taught to feel that mankind depends upon them, and that they owe benevolent service especially to the less fortunate classes beneath them. But let it not be supposed that they will be prigs—far from it. They will turn off with a deprecating laugh any too portentous remark that puts into explicit words what they will all believe in their hearts. Their manners will be easy and pleasant, and their sense of humour unfailing.

The latest stage in the education of the most intellectual of the governing class will consist of training for research. Research will be highly organized, and young people will not be allowed to choose what particular piece of research they shall do. They will, of course, be directed to research in those subjects for which they have shown special ability. A great deal of scientific knowledge will be concealed from all but a few. There will be arcana reserved for a priestly class of researchers, who will be carefully selected for their combination of brains with loyalty. One may, I think, expect that research will be much more technical than fundamental. The men at the head of any department of research will be elderly, and content to think that the fundamentals of their subject are sufficiently known. Discoveries which upset the official view of fundamentals, if they are made by young men, will incur disfavour, and if rashly published will lead to degradation. Young men to whom any fundamental innovation occurs will make cautious attempts to persuade their professors to view the new ideas with favour, but if these attempts fail they will conceal their new ideas until they themselves have acquired positions of authority, by which time they will probably have forgotten them. The atmosphere of authority and organization will be extremely favourable to technical research, but somewhat inimical to such subversive innovations as have been seen, for example, in physics during the present century. There will be, of course, an official metaphysic, which will be regarded as intellectually unimportant but politically sacrosanct. In the long run, the rate of scientific progress will diminish, and discovery will be killed by respect for authority.

As for the manual workers, they will be discouraged from serious thought: they will be made as comfortable as possible, and their hours of work will be much shorter than they are at present; they will have no fear of destitution or of misfortune to their children. As soon as working hours are over, amusements will be provided, of a sort calculated to cause wholesome mirth, and to prevent any thoughts of discontent which otherwise might cloud their happiness.

On those rare occasions when a boy or girl who has passed the age at which it is usual to determine social status shows such marked ability as to seem the intellectual equal of the rulers, a difficult situation will arise, requiring serious consideration. If the youth is content to abandon his previous associates and to throw in his lot whole-heartedly with the rulers, he may, after suitable tests, be promoted, but if he shows any regrettable solidarity with his previous associates, the rulers will reluctantly conclude that there is nothing to be done with him except to send him to the lethal chamber before his ill-disciplined intelligence has had time to spread revolt. This will be a painful duty to the rulers, but I think they will not shrink from performing it.

In normal cases, children of sufficiently excellent heredity will be admitted to the governing class from the moment of conception. I start with this moment rather than with birth, since it is from this moment and not merely from the moment of birth that the treatment of the two classes will be different. If, however, by the time the child reaches the age of three, it is fairly clear that he does not attain the required standard, he will be degraded at that point. I assume that by that time it will be possible to judge of the intelligence of a child of three with a fair measure of accuracy. Cases in which there is doubt, which should, however, be few, will be subjected to careful observation up to the age of six, at which moment one supposes the official decision will be possible except in a few rare instances. Conversely, children born of manual workers may be promoted at any moment between the age of three and six, but only in quite rare instances at later ages. I think it may be assumed, however, that there would be a very strong tendency for the governing class to become hereditary, and that after a few generations not many children would be moved from either class into the other. This is especially likely to be the case if embryological methods of improving the breed are applied to the governing class, but not to the others. In this way the gulf between the two classes as regards native intelligence may become continually wider and wider. This will not lead to the abolition of the less intelligent class, since the rulers will not wish to undertake uninteresting manual work, or to be deprived of the opportunity for exercising benevolence and public spirit which they derive from the management of the manual workers.

CHAPTER XVI

Scientific Reproduction

SCIENCE, when it has once acquired a firm hold upon social organization, is hardly likely to stop short at those biological aspects of human life which have hitherto been left to the joint guidance of religion and instinct. We may, I think, assume that both the quantity and the quality of the population will be carefully regulated by the State, but that sexual intercourse apart from children will be regarded as a private matter so long as it is not allowed to interfere with work. As regards quantity, the State statisticians will determine as carefully as they can whether the population of the world at the moment is above or below the number which leads to the greatest material comfort per head. They will also take account of all such changes of technique as can be foreseen. No doubt the usual rule will be to aim at a stationary population, but if some important invention, such as artificial food, should greatly cheapen the production of necessaries, an increase of population might for a time be thought wise. I shall, however, assume that, in normal times, the world government will decree a stationary population.

If we were right in supposing that the scientific society will have different social grades according to the kind of work to be performed, we may assume also that it will have uses for human beings who are not of the highest grade of intelligence. It is probable that there will be certain kinds of labour mainly performed by negroes, and that manual workers in general will be bred for patience and muscle rather than for brains. The governors and experts, on the contrary, will be bred chiefly for their intellectual powers and their strength of character. Assuming that both kinds of breeding are scientifically carried out, there will come to be an increasing divergence between the two types, making them in the end almost different species.

Scientific breeding, in any truly scientific form, would at present encounter insuperable obstacles both from religion and from sentiment. To carry it out scientifically it would be necessary, as among domestic animals, to employ only a small percentage of males for purposes of breeding. It may be thought that religion and sentiment will always succeed in opposing an immovable veto to such a system. I wish I could think so. But I believe that sentiment is quite extraordinarily plastic, and that the individualistic religion to which we have been accustomed is likely to be increasingly replaced by a religion of devotion to the State. Among Russian Communists this has already happened. In any case, what is demanded is scarcely as difficult a control of natural impulses as is involved in the celibacy of the Catholic priesthood. Wherever remarkable achievements are possible and are at the same time such as to satisfy men's moral idealism, the love of power is capable of swallowing up the instinctive life of the affections, especially if an outlet is permitted to purely physical sexual impulses. Traditional religion, which has been violently dispossessed in Russia, will suffer a setback everywhere if the Russian experiment proves successful. In any case its outlook is difficult to reconcile with that of industrialism and scientific technique. Traditional religion was based upon a sense of man's impotence in the face of natural forces, whereas scientific technique induces a sense of the impotence of natural forces in the face of man's intelligence. Combined with this sense of power, a certain degree of austerity in regard to the softer pleasures is quite natural. One sees it already in many of those who are creating the mechanistic society of the future. In America this austerity has taken the form of Protestant piety, in Russia of devotion to Communism.

I think, therefore, that there is hardly any limit to the departures from traditional sentiment which science may introduce into the question of reproduction. If the simultaneous regulation of quantity and quality is taken seriously in the future, we may expect that in each generation some 25 per cent. of women and some 5 per cent. of men will be selected to be the parents of the next generation, while the remainder of the population will be sterilized, which will in no way interfere with their sexual pleasures, but will merely render these pleasures destitute of social importance. The women who are selected for breeding will have to have eight or nine children each, but will not be expected to perform any other work except the suckling of the children for a suitable number of months. No obstacles will be placed upon their relations with sterile men, or upon the relations of sterile men and women with each other, but reproduction will be regarded as a matter which concerns the State, and will not be left to the free choice of the persons concerned. Perhaps it will be found that artificial impregnation is more certain and less embarrassing, since it will obviate the need of any personal contact between the father and mother of the prospective child. Sentiments of personal affection may still be connected with intercourse not intended to be fruitful, while impregnation will be regarded in an entirely different manner, more in the light of a surgical operation, so that it will be thought not ladylike to have it performed in the natural manner. The qualities for which parents will be chosen will differ greatly according to the status which it is hoped the child will occupy. In the governing class a considerable degree of intelligence will be demanded of parents; perfect health will, of course, be indispensable. So long as gestation is allowed to persist to its natural period, mothers will also have to be selected by their capacity for easy delivery, and will therefore have to be free from an unduly narrow pelvis. It is probable, however, that as time goes on the period of gestation will be shortened, and the later months of foetal development will take place in an incubator. This would also free mothers from the need of suckling their children, and would thus make maternity a not very onerous matter. The care of infants intended to belong to the governing class would seldom be left to the mothers. Mothers would be selected by their eugenic qualities, and these would not necessarily be the qualities required in a nurse. On the other hand, the early months of pregnancy might be more burdensome than at present, since the fœtus would be subjected to various kinds of scientific treatment intended to affect beneficially not only its own characteristics but those of its possible descendants.

Fathers would, of course, have nothing to do with their own children. There would be in general only one father to every five mothers, and it is quite likely that he would never have even seen the mothers of his children. The sentiment of paternity would thus disappear completely. Probably in time the same thing would happen, though to a slightly less degree, in regard to mothers. If birth were prematurely induced, and the child separated from its mother at birth, maternal sentiment would have little chance to develop.

Among the workers it is probable that less elaborate care would be taken, since it is easier to breed for muscle than to breed for brains, and it is not unlikely that women would be allowed to bring up their own children in the old-fashioned natural manner. There would not be, among the workers, the same need as among the governors for fanatical devotion to the State, and there would not be, therefore, on the part of the government, the same jealousy of the private affections. Among the governors, one must suppose, all private sentiments would be viewed with suspicion. A man and woman who showed any ardent devotion to each other would be regarded as they are at present regarded by moralists when they are not married. There would be professional nurses in *crêches*, and professional teachers in nursery schools, but they would be considered to be failing in their duty if they felt any special affection for special children. Children who showed any special affection for a particular adult would be separated from that adult. Ideas of this kind are already widespread; they will be found suggested, for example, in Dr. John B. Watson's book on education.[1] The tendency of the scientific manipulator is to regard all private affections as unfortunate. Freudians have shown us that they are the sources of complexes. Administrators realize that they stand in the way of a whole-hearted devotion to business. The Church sanctioned certain kinds of love while condemning others, but the modern ascetic is more thoroughgoing, and condemns all kinds of love equally as mere folly and waste of time.

What should we expect of the mental make-up of people in such a world? The manual workers may, I think, be fairly happy. One may assume that the rulers will be successful in making the manual workers foolish and frivolous; work will not be too severe, and there will be endless amusements of a trivial sort. Owing to sterilization, love affairs need not have awkward consequences so long as they are not between a man and woman who are

[1] Cf. *Psychological Care of Infant and Child,* by John B. Watson, p. 83.

both of them unsterilized. In this way a life of easygoing and frivolous pleasure may be provided for the manual workers, combined of course with a superstitious reverence for the governors instilled in childhood and prolonged by the propaganda to which adults will be exposed.

The psychology of the governors will be a more difficult matter. They will be expected to display an arduous and hard-working devotion to the ideal of the scientific State, and to sacrifice to this ideal all the softer sentiments such as love of wife and children. Friendships between fellow-workers, whether of the same or of different sexes, will tend to become ardent, and will not infrequently overstep the limits which the public moralists will have fixed. In such a case the authorities will separate the friends, unless in doing so they will interrupt some important research or administrative undertaking. When for some such public reason friends are not separated, they will be admonished. By means of governmental microphones the censors will listen-in to their conversations, and if these should at any time become tinged with sentiment, disciplinary measures will be adopted. All the deeper feelings will be frustrated, with the sole exception of devotion to science and the State.

The governors will, of course, have their amusements for leisure hours. I do not see how art or literature could flourish in such a world, nor do I think that the emotions from which they spring and to which they appeal would meet with governmental approval, but athletics of a strenuous kind will be encouraged among the young of the governing class, and dangerous sports will be considered valuable as a training in those habits of mind and body by which authority over the manual workers will be maintained. Love-making among the sterilized will be subjected to no restrictions either of law or of public opinion, but it will be casual and temporary, involving none of the deeper feelings and no serious affection. Persons suffering from unendurable boredom will be encouraged to ascend Mount Everest or fly over the South Pole, but the need for such distractions will be regarded as a sign of mental or physical ill-health.

In such a world, though there may be pleasure, there will be no joy. The result will be a type displaying the usual characteristics of vigorous ascetics. They will be harsh and unbending, tending towards cruelty in their ideals and their readiness to consider that the infliction of pain is necessary for the public good. I do not imagine that pain will be much inflicted as punishment for sin, since no sin will be recognized except insubordination and failure to carry out the purposes of the State. It is more probable that the sadistic impulses which the asceticism will generate will find their outlet in scientific experiment. The advancement of knowledge will be held to justify much torture of individuals by surgeons, biochemists, and experimental psychologists. As time goes on the amount of added knowledge required to justify a given amount of pain will diminish, and the number of governors attracted to the kinds of research necessitating cruel experiments will increase. Just as the sun worship of the Aztecs demanded the painful death of thousands of human beings annually, so the new scientific religion will demand its holocausts of sacred victims. Gradually the world will grow more dark and more terrible. Strange perversions of instinct will first lurk in the dark corners and then gradually overwhelm the men in high places. Sadistic pleasures will not suffer the moral condemnation that will be meted out to the softer joys, since, like the persecutions of the Inquisition, they will be found in harmony with the prevailing asceticism. In the end such a system must break down either in an orgy of bloodshed or in the rediscovery of joy.

Such at least is the only ray of hope to lighten the darkness of these visions of Cassandra, but perhaps in permitting this ray of hope we have allowed ourselves to yield to a foolish optimism. Perhaps by means of injections and drugs and chemicals the population could be induced to bear whatever its scientific masters may decide to be for its good. New forms of drunkenness involving no subsequent headache may be discovered, and new forms of intoxication may be invented so delicious that for their sakes men are willing to pass their sober hours in misery. All these are possibilities in a world governed by knowledge without love, and power without delight. The man drunk with power is destitute of wisdom, and so long as he rules the world, the world will be a place devoid of beauty and of joy.

CHAPTER XVII

Science and Values

THE scientific society which has been sketched in the chapters of this Part is, of course, not to be taken altogether as serious prophecy. It is an attempt to depict the world which would result if scientific technique were to rule unchecked. The reader will have observed that features that everyone would consider desirable are almost inextricably mingled with features that are repulsive. The reason of this is that we have been imagining a society developed in accordance with certain ingredients of human nature to the exclusion of all others. As ingredients they are good; as the sole driving force they are likely to be disastrous. The impulse towards scientific construction is admirable when it does not thwart any of the major impulses that give value to human life, but when it is allowed to forbid all outlet to everything but itself it becomes a form of cruel tyranny. There is, I think, a real danger lest the world should become subject to a tyranny of this sort, and it is on this account that I have not shrunk from depicting the darker features of the world that scientific manipulation unchecked might wish to create.

Science in the course of the few centuries of its history has undergone an internal development which appears to be not yet completed. One may sum up this development as the passage from contemplation to manipulation. The love of knowledge to which the growth of science is due is itself the product of a twofold impulse. We may seek knowledge of an object because we love the object or because we wish to have power over it. The former impulse leads to the kind of knowledge that is contemplative, the latter to the kind that is practical. In the development of science the power impulse has increasingly prevailed over the love impulse. The power impulse is embodied in industrialism and in governmental technique. It is embodied also in the philosophies known as pragmatism and instrumentalism. Each of these philosophies holds, broadly speaking, that our beliefs about any object are true in so far as they enable us to manipulate it with advantage to ourselves. This is what may be called a governmental view of truth. Of truth so conceived science offers us a great deal; indeed there seems no limit to its possible triumphs. To the man who wishes to change his environment science offers astonishingly powerful tools, and if knowledge consists in the power to produce intended changes, then science gives knowledge in abundance.

But the desire for knowledge has another form, belonging to an entirely different set of emotions. The mystic, the lover, and the poet are also seekers after knowledge—not perhaps very successful seekers, but none the less worthy of respect on that account. In all forms of love we wish to have knowledge of what is loved, not for purposes of power, but for the ecstasy of contemplation. "In knowledge of God standeth our eternal life," but not because knowledge of God gives us power over Him. Wherever there is ecstasy or joy or delight derived from an object there is the desire to know that object—to know it not in the manipulative fashion that consists of turning it into something else, but to know it in the fashion of the beatific vision, because in itself and for itself it sheds happiness upon the lover. In sex love as in other forms of love the impulse to this kind of knowledge exists, unless the love is purely physical or practical. This may indeed be made the touchstone of any love that is valuable. Love which has value contains an impulse towards that kind of knowledge out of which the mystic union springs.

Science in its beginnings was due to men who were in love with the world. They perceived the beauty of the stars and the sea, of the winds and the mountains. Because they loved them their thoughts dwelt upon them, and they wished to understand them more intimately than a mere outward contemplation made possible. "The world," said Heraclitus, "is an ever-living fire, with measures kindling and measures going out." Heraclitus and the other Ionian philosophers, from whom came the first impulse to scientific knowledge, felt the strange beauty of the world almost like a madness in the blood. They were men of Titanic passionate intellect, and from the intensity of their intellectual passion the whole movement of the modern world has sprung. But step by step, as science has developed, the impulse of love which gave it birth has been increasingly thwarted, while the impulse of power, which was at first a mere camp-follower, has gradually usurped command in virtue of its unforeseen success. The lover of nature has been baffled, the tyrant over nature has been rewarded. As physics has developed, it has deprived us step by step of what we thought we knew concerning the intimate nature of the physical world. Colour and sound, light and shade, form and texture, belong no longer to that external nature that the Ionians sought as the bride of their devotion. All these things have been transferred from the beloved to the lover, and the beloved has become a skeleton of rattling bones, cold and dreadful, but perhaps a mere phantasm. The poor physicists, appalled at the desert that their formulae have revealed, call upon God to give them comfort, but God must share the ghostliness of His creation, and the answer that the physicists think they hear to their cry is only the frightened beating of their own hearts. Disappointed as the lover of nature, the man of science is becoming its tyrant. What matters it, says the practical man, whether the outer world exists or is a dream, provided I can make it behave as I wish? Thus science has more and more substituted power-knowledge for love-knowledge, and as this substitution becomes completed science tends more and more to become sadistic. The scientific society of the future as we have been imagining it is one in which the power impulse has completely overwhelmed the impulse of love, and this is the psychological source of the cruelties which it is in danger of exhibiting.

Science, which began as the pursuit of truth, is becoming incompatible with veracity, since complete veracity tends more and more to complete scientific scepticism. When science is considered contemplatively, not practically, we find that what we believe we believe owing to animal faith, and it is only our disbeliefs that are due to science. When, on the other hand, science is considered as a technique for the transformation of ourselves and our environment, it is found to give us a power quite independent of its metaphysical validity. But we can only wield this power by ceasing to ask ourselves metaphysical questions as to the nature of reality. Yet these questions are the evidence of a lover's attitude towards the world. Thus it is only in so far as we renounce the world as its lovers that we can conquer it as its technicians. But this division in the soul is fatal to what is best in man. As soon as the failure of science considered as metaphysics is realized, the power conferred by science as a technique is only obtainable by something analogous to the worship of Satan, that is to say, by the renunciation of love.

This is the fundamental reason why the prospect of a scientific society must be viewed with apprehension. The scientific society in its pure form, which is what we have been trying to depict, is incompatible with the pursuit of truth, with love, with art, with spontaneous delight, with every ideal that men have hitherto cherished, with the sole exception of ascetic renunciation. It is not knowledge that is the source of these dangers. Knowledge is good and ignorance is evil: to this principle the lover of the world can admit no exception. Nor is it power in and for itself that is the source of danger. What is dangerous is power wielded for the sake of power, not power wielded for the sake of genuine good. The leaders of the modern world are drunk with power: the fact that they can do something that no one previously thought it possible to do is to them a sufficient reason for doing it. Power is not one of the ends of life, but merely a means to other ends, and until men remember the ends that power should subserve, science will not do what it might to minister to the good life. But what then are the ends of life, the reader will say. I do not think that one man has a right to legislate for another on this matter. For each individual the ends of life are those things which he deeply desires, and which if they existed would give him peace. Or, if it be thought that peace is too much to ask this side of the grave, let us say that the ends of life should give delight or joy or ecstasy. In the conscious desires of the man who seeks power for its own sake there is something dusty: when he has it he wants only more power, and does not find rest in contemplation of what he has. The lover, the poet and the mystic find a fuller satisfaction than the seeker after power can ever know, since they can rest in the object of their love, whereas the seeker after power must be perpetually engaged in some fresh manipulation if he is not to suffer from a sense of emptiness. I think therefore that the satisfactions of the lover, using that word in its broad-

est sense, exceed the satisfactions of the tyrant, and deserve a higher place among the ends of life. When I come
to die I shall not feel that I have lived in vain. I have
seen the earth turn red at evening, the dew sparkling in
the morning, and the snow shining under a frosty sun; I
have smelt rain after drought, and have heard the stormy
Atlantic beat upon the granite shores of Cornwall. Science may bestow these and other joys upon more people
than could otherwise enjoy them. If so, its power will be
wisely used. But when it takes out of life the moments to
which life owes its value, science will not deserve admira-
tion, however cleverly and however elaborately it may
lead men along the road to despair. The sphere of values
lies outside science, except in so far as science consists in
the pursuit of knowledge. Science as the pursuit of power
must not obtrude upon the sphere of values, and scientific
technique, if it is to enrich human life, must not outweigh
the ends which it should serve.

The number of men who determine the character of an
age is small. Columbus, Luther and Charles V dominated
the sixteenth century; Galileo and Descartes governed
the seventeenth. The important men in the age that is
just ended are Edison, Rockefeller, Lenin, and Sun Yat-
sen. With the exception of Sun Yat-sen these were men
devoid of culture, contemptuous of the past, self-
confident, and ruthless. Traditional wisdom had no place
in their thoughts and feelings; mechanism and organization were what interested them. A different education
might have made all these men quite different. Edison

might in his youth have acquired a knowledge of history and poetry and art; Rockefeller might have been taught how he had been anticipated by Crœsus and Crassus; Lenin, instead of having hatred implanted in him by the execution of his brother during his student days, might have made himself acquainted with the rise of Islam and the development of Puritanism from piety to plutocracy. By means of such an education some little leaven of doubt might have entered the souls of these great men. Given a little doubt their achievement would perhaps have been less in volume, but much greater in value.

Our world has a heritage of culture and beauty, but unfortunately we have been handing on this heritage only to the less active and important members of each generation. The government of the world, by which I do not mean its ministerial posts but its key-positions of power, has been allowed to fall into the hands of men ignorant of the past, without tenderness towards what is traditional, without understanding of what they are destroying. There is no essential reason why this should be the case. To prevent it is an educational problem, and not a very difficult one. Men in the past were often parochial in space, but the dominant men of our age are parochial in time. They feel for the past a contempt that it does not deserve, and for the present a respect that it deserves still less. The copy-book maxims of a former age have become outworn, but a new set of copy-book maxims is required. First among these I should put: "It is better to do a little good than much harm." To give content to this maxim it would of course be necessary to instil some sense of what is good. Few men in the present day, for example, can be induced to believe that there is no inherent excellence in rapid locomotion. To climb from Hell to Heaven is good, though it be a slow and laborious process; to fall from Heaven to Hell is bad, even though it be done with the speed of Milton's Satan. Nor can it be said that a mere increase in the production of material commodities is in itself a thing of great value. To prevent extreme poverty is important, but to add to the possessions of those who already have too much is a worthless waste of effort. To prevent crime may be necessary, but to invent new crimes in order than the police may show skill in preventing them is less admirable. The new powers that science has given to man can only be wielded safely by those who, whether through the study of history or through their own experience of life, have acquired some reverence for human feelings and some tenderness towards the emotions that give colour to the daily existence of men and women. I do not mean to deny that scientific technique may in time build an artificial world in every way preferable to that in which men have hitherto lived, but I do say that if this is to be done it must be done tentatively and with a realization that the purpose of government is not merely to afford pleasure to those who govern, but to make life tolerable for those who are governed. Scientific technique must no longer be allowed to form the whole culture of the holders of power, and it must become an essential part of men's ethical outlook to realize that the will alone cannot make a good life. Knowing and feeling are equally essential ingredients both in the life of the individual and in that of the community. Knowledge, if it is wide and intimate, brings with it a realization of distant times and places, an awareness that the individual is not omnipotent or all-important, and a perspective in which values are seen more clearly than by those to whom a distant view is impossible. Even more important than knowledge is the life of the emotions. A world without delight and without affection is a world destitute of value. These things the scientific manipulator must remember, and if he does his manipulation may be wholly beneficial. All that is needed is that men should not be so intoxicated by new power as to forget the truths that were familiar to every previous generation. Not all wisdom is new, nor is all folly out of date.

Man has been disciplined hitherto by his subjection to nature. Having emancipated himself from this subjection, he is showing something of the defects of slave-turned-master. A new moral outlook is called for in which submission to the powers of nature is replaced by respect for what is best in man. It is where this respect is lacking that scientific technique is dangerous. So long as it is present, science, having delivered man from bondage to nature, can proceed to deliver him from bondage to the slavish part of himself. The dangers exist, but they are not inevitable, and hope for the future is at least as rational as fear.

THE END

INDEX

Index

THE NORTON LIBRARY

Abrams, M. H.: *The Mirror and the Lamp: Romantic Theory and the Critical Tradition.* N102

Aron, Raymond: *The Opium of the Intellectuals.* N106

Austen, Jane, *Persuasion,* Introduction by David Daiches. N163

Boas, Franz, *Anthropology and Modern Life.* N104

Brill, A. A., *Freud's Contribution to Psychiatry.* N511

Browning, Robert, *The Ring and the Book,* Introduction by Wylie Sypher. N105

Clifford, Henry S., *The City Poem,* Prologue, New preface and epilogue. N174

Corrie, Hernando, *The Reformation,* and Introduction by Howard Mumford. N160

Drew, Elizabeth, *Discovering Poetry.* N110

Eliade, Mircea, *Myth and the Real.* N105

Freeling, Alfred, *Essays on Music.* N177

Erikson, Erik H., *Young Man Luther.* N170

Ferrero, Guglielmo, *The Life of Caesar.* N111

Fielding, Henry, *Joseph Andrews,* Intro. by Mary Ellen Chase. N83

Freud, Sigmund, *The Ego and The Id.* N142

Freud, Sigmund, *Civilization and its Discontents.* N158

Gaskell, Mrs. Elizabeth, *Mary Barton,* Introduction by Myron F. Brightfield. N175

Gorer, Geoffrey, *Africa Dances,* New Intro. N173

Gorer, Geoffrey and John Rickman, M.D., *The People of Great Russia.* N112

Hartman, Edith, *Speakman the Genesis.* N179

Hamilton, Edith, *The Greek Way.* N110

Hauser, Arnold, *The Social History of Art.* N114

Holmes, Karen, *Are You Considering Psychoanalysis?* N131

Huxley, Aldous, *Texts and Pretexts.* N114

James, William, *Pragmatism and Four Essays from The Meaning of Truth.* N115

Jung, Paul, *Psychology.* N115

THE NORTON LIBRARY

478